JANE W. GRANT

IN THE STEPS OF EXCEPTIONAL WOMEN

THE STORY OF THE FAWCETT SOCIETY
1866–2016

Francis
Boutle
Publishers

First published by Francis Boutle Publishers
272 Alexandra Park Road
London N22 7BG
Tel/Fax: (020) 8889 7744
Email: info@francisboutle.co.uk
www.francisboutle.co.uk

ISBN 978 0 9935344 1 6

Contents

Dedication

Recently I came across a Fawcett Society newsletter dated March 1981. Mary Stott was chairman (*sic*) and, following on from the speech which Kathleen Halpin had given at the commemoration service that year, Mary wrote:

> Many members of the society … feel strongly that we need a history of our work and endeavours during the period following the winning of the vote on equal terms, in 1928, up to the present day. If any member reading this feels inspired to do research into our past history, we should be very glad to hear.

I'm sorry I never got to discuss this project with Mary (although I discussed much else with her during long afternoons in her flat in Blackheath) and that it has taken nearly thirty-five years to come to fruition. But, Mary, here it is. This is dedicated to you and to all the other exceptional women – including Sandy Shulman★ who coined the phrase – who have devoted their time and campaigning passion to Fawcett and to whom the Society owes an immeasurable debt.

This book is also dedicated to my sister Charlotte and my daughter Tara, two more exceptional women.

★ Sandy Shulman, 'We walk in the footsteps of some exceptional women', Annual Report of the Fawcett Society, 1987-88.

List of illustrations

Figures

Acknowledgements

Although I have used other libraries (such as the Parliamentary Archives and the Library of the Museum of London) the research for this book has been overwhelmingly undertaken in the archives of the Women's Library (formerly the Fawcett Library and, before that, the Women's Service Library), which holds the Fawcett archives. I am accordingly hugely grateful to the staff of the Women's Library, whether in Old Castle Street or latterly in the Women's Library Reading Room at the London School of Economics (and those like Indy Bhullar, Sonia Gomez and Gillian Murphy who moved from one to the other) for their patient support and help in locating archives from a collection that is both enormous and very far from fully catalogued. (I have acknowledged my use of particular archives in the relevant sections of the text.) The Women's Library and its staff, especially Anna Towlson, Archives and Special Collections manager, and Kate Higgins, have also given invaluable assistance in locating and releasing many of the illustrations in this book. I am thrilled that Nicola Wright, Anna Towlson, Martin Reid and Eleanor Payne from the LSE Library have committed themselves to celebrating Fawcett's 150th birthday by fully cataloguing the Society's archives and mounting an exhibition. Future researchers will be able to write much better books!

The Fawcett Society and their members and supporters have been constantly bothered by me and have been extremely generous in their response both with materials and with memories, views, and suggestions. The list that follows is in the order in which they appear in the book: Sandy Shulman, Ann Dingsdale, Elizabeth Crawford, Helen Kay, Jill Liddington, David Doughan, Maureen Castens, Anne Summers, Miriam David, Mary Richardson, Zoë Fairbairns, A. E. L Davis, Lesley Abdela, Margaret Joachim, Lily Segerman-Peck, Annette Lawson, Margaret Laird, Antonia Byatt, Shelagh Diplock, Mary-Ann Stephenson, Jane Esuantsiwa Goldsmith, Janet Scott, Jenny Watson, Katherine Rake, Sue Tibballs, Belinda Phipps, Jenni Murray and Sam Smethers.

I am grateful to my friend Jo Rogers for access to her great-aunt Marion's scrapbook and for photographs of Aldeburgh, to Olivia Lambert for her invaluable help with pictures, and to Mike Locke, then of the Centre for Institutional Studies at the University of East London, for encouraging this book into existence. I also thank Charlotte Gere,

Clare Wright (of Wright and Wright Architects) and Henrietta Phipps for their kind agreement to reproduction of images. Elin Medalen, Doris Amankwaah and Darinka Aleksic, all of the Fawcett Society, have given invaluable help. Thanks are also due to my publisher Clive Boutle for his interest and support and to Kate Tattersall, who drew the chart at page 24-25. Every effort has been made to identify holders of copyright in the material used, but if any infringement has occurred, the author will be glad to correct this in any future editions of the book.

My gratitude goes too to my long-suffering family (especially my husband Neville for endlessly finding things). But my most heartfelt thanks must go to Susan Pares, the book's editor and picture editor. Susan is skilled, patient and kind in equal measure, even when my sight was failing and I lost everything. This book would not have been finished without her. It is her book as much as mine (although any faults are of course my own).

Finally, great thanks to Westminster School, and particularly to Elizabeth Wells and Peter Chequer, for welcoming us into the Millicent Fawcett Hall for the launch of this book.

Jane Grant

Picture acknowledgements

Author's collection: 30, 44, 46, 55
City of London Polytechnic/London Metropolitan University: 42, 45
Peter Cook/VIEW: 43
The Fawcett Society: 47, 50, 51, 52, 53, 54, 56, 57, 58, 59
Jim Hoare: 26
Estate of Henry Lamb: 47
London Borough of Lambeth, Archives Department: 3
Susan Pares: 3
Punch Ltd.: 5
Alan Reevell: 48
Jo Rogers: 1
The Times/News Syndication: 34
Westminster City Archives: 33
The Women's Library@LSE: Frontispiece, 2, 4, 6, 7, 8, 9, 10, 11, 12, 13, 14, 15, 16, 17, 18, 19, 20, 21, 22, 23, 24, 25, 27, 28, 29, 31, 32, 35, 36, 37, 38, 39, 40, 41, 49

fawcett
demands a
fair deal for
women
fawcett
www.fawcettsociety.org.uk

Preface

A hundred and fifty years ago, in 1866, a young woman from Suffolk helped to collect signatures for John Stuart Mill, the political economist, philosopher and MP and author of *The Subjection of Women*, for his suffrage amendment to the Reform Bill. Her name was Millicent Garrett and she was in fact too young, at nineteen, to sign the petition herself. Nor was the Women's Suffrage petition, for which 1,499 signatures were collected, successful. The Reform Bill went through without the amendment or any mention of women's voting rights. It was to take sixty-two years, till 1928, until the full vote was won.

But the petition of 1866 set in train a series of actions which were to lead, inexorably though slowly and certainly not straightforwardly, to women's suffrage. Although many, many people were involved in this struggle, the role of Millicent Garrett Fawcett (as she became after her marriage to the Liberal politician Henry Fawcett in 1867) was pivotal. She was the thread that held the struggle together over time; she was there in the Ladies Gallery of the House of Commons to see Mill's amendment presented and defeated in 1867 and again in the House of Lords in 1928 for the passing of the Equal Franchise Act, which at last gave women the vote on the same basis as men. The organisation she nurtured eventually came, in 1953, to be named after her and the Fawcett Society, sustained by new generations of activists, remains at the cutting edge of the fight for women's rights today, 150 years after Millicent first took action. This book is the story of that organisation.

January 2016

1. Alde House, Aldeburgh, where Millicent Fawcett was brought up

In the beginning

If you climb the stairs to reach the upper tiers of the Concert Hall at the Maltings in Snape in Suffolk, you pass on the landing six rather dim paintings. Four of them are of the maltsters who used to work in the original maltings in the second half of the nineteenth century. The last two are of Newson Garrett and his wife Louisa, who, according to the inscription, 'built the Maltings in the first half of the nineteenth century'. These were Millicent's parents.

The Garretts were an important Suffolk family. Newson's elder brother Richard operated the renowned machinery works at Leiston (now transformed into the Long Shop Museum), while Newson ran a successful corn and coal merchant's business at Snape Bridge before developing the Maltings nearby. These profitable ventures established Newson firmly in the middle classes of Aldeburgh, a small town on the coast of Suffolk, where he brought up his family. Over time the Garretts were to occupy several houses around Aldeburgh including Alde House and, once grown up, the children would keep holiday houses there and thus keep returning all their lives. Elizabeth Garrett Anderson, Millicent's sister, retained strong enough ties with Aldeburgh to be elected its mayor in 1908, the first woman in England to be elected to such office.

Millicent, her three older sisters Agnes, Louisa and Elizabeth, and her cousin Rhoda, were unusual in that they were given an education. In Millicent's case she was sent to a private boarding school in Blackheath from 1858 to 1863, until the money gave out when she was fifteen This school was run by the poet Robert Browning's aunt, Louisa Browning, and, again, unusually for contemporary girls' schools, gave Millicent 'quickened intellectual interests'.[1] The Garrett girls appear to have been brought up at home in an atmosphere of considerable high-mindedness and purpose, strengthened by the frequent presence of Elizabeth's great friend Emily Davies and by a free-thinking father. Millicent Garrett seems to have been destined for great things from an early age. There is a nice story that her sister Elizabeth and Emily Davies were, as young women, sitting round the fire in Aldeburgh one night deciding how they would further the women's cause, while Millicent sat quietly in the corner. Emily said decisively: "'...Well, it is clear enough what is to be done; You, Elizabeth, must open the Medical Profession to women'" (which of course she did), "'I must see about Higher Education'" (which

of course she did, including founding Girton College at Cambridge)'", and as the vote will follow after the other two, Milly here, who is younger than we are, must attend to that'".[2] As, of course, she did.

It was Emily Davies who introduced Elizabeth to Barbara Bodichon, Jessie Boucherett, Bessie Rayner Parkes, Isa Craig and the other 'ladies of Langham Place', possibly the earliest group of feminists in England. They ran a Women's Employment Bureau and from 1858 to 1864 produced the *English Woman's Journal* from a small office in 19 Langham Place in central London. This also acted as a Ladies' Institute, 'a place of rest and recreation for London's many middle-class working women'.[3] As Sheila Herstein puts it, '[n]ever before had a group of women met together in England to discuss and organise political action to change the status of the sex'.[4] The Langham Place Ladies also formed an important part of the Kensington Society, which was very influential in the development of the women's suffrage movement.

These women were to inspire Elizabeth's protracted struggle to qualify as a doctor – a struggle much helped and spurred on by her meeting in 1859 with Dr Elizabeth Blackwell, who had qualified as a doctor in the United States, and a struggle much supported throughout by their father Newson rather than their mother, who did not approve. As Milly grew up and went to London more often to stay with her married sister Louisa Smith, she also came under the influence of the ladies of Langham Place. For instance, in 1865 she was taken to one of the election meetings held by John Stuart Mill who had been invited to stand for Parliament for the City of Westminster. With Mill's election 'the right of women to enfranchisement became a practical political issue for the first time'[5] and for Milly this meeting was mind-changing: it 'kindled tenfold my enthusiasm for women's suffrage'.[6]

It was also in 1865 that Milly was to meet Henry Fawcett, the blind Cambridge academic and Liberal candidate for the parliamentary seat of Brighton, a friend of Mill's

and renowned for his radical-ism as much as for his disabil-ity. There were some family obstacles raised to their mar-riage, mainly to do with his blindness, but these were over-come, and in 1867 the wedding took place, the start of an extremely happy marriage, one based very much on mutual support. If Milly acted as her husband's 'eyes', he was able to open political doors for her and support her as she went bravely through them.

Milly had in 1866 become increasingly involved in suffragist politics. Once Mill was elected, the ladies of Langham Place, together with Emily Davies and Elizabeth and Millicent Garrett, got together to form a very small, informal committee (known as the Women's Suffrage Committee) to promote a pro-suffragist petition that Mill was pre-pared to present to Parliament as part of the discussion of the Reform Bill. This amend-ment called for "'[t]he representation of all householders, without distinction of sex, who possess such property or rental qualifications as your honourable House may determine'".7

The office for this campaign was in the drawing room of Elizabeth's house in Upper Berkeley Street, and although Millicent was not considered, at nineteen, old enough

3. 51 The Lawn, home of Millicent and Henry Fawcett, 1874-84. Watercolour by J. V. Thompson, 1885. Below: Plaque commemorating their house, installed 2013 in Vauxhall Park

actually to sign the petition herself, she campaigned tirelessly for others to do so. In the end 1,499 signatures (an impressive total in a pre-digital age) were collected and these were presented to Mill – a moment recorded in a painting by Bertha Newcombe in 1910. The scene is set in Westminster Hall and the petition is being pulled out from its hiding place under the apple-seller's table and handed over to Mill by Elizabeth Garrett and Emily Davies.[8]

Nonetheless, this early piece of organising ended in failure. The petition, presented in June 1866, was rejected. An amendment to the Reform Bill, presented by Mill in 1867, which intended to substitute the word 'person' for the word 'man', was not passed, although the debate around it 'brought the subject into the full blare of publicity and launched it definitely upon the political field'.[9] Millicent went to hear the debate in the inhospitable Ladies Gallery in the House of Commons and was struck by the 'evidently powerful impression the speech made on the House'.[10] It was to launch Millicent on a lifetime of campaigning for the suffrage.

The immediate consequence of this debate was the establishment of the first Women's Suffrage Committee in London, run from Mentia Taylor's house, with its first meeting in July 1867. In spite of the fact that she was newly married to a man who badly needed her support, that she had to run houses in both Cambridge and London and in 1868 had a baby daughter Philippa to look after, Millicent was an active member of this committee and did not flinch from what Ray Strachey saw as the challenges of a movement that 'even at that early stage…was hedged about with difficulties'.[11] Problems were many: from a lack of understanding of the strength of opposition to what they were proposing – and hence how long it might take – to a lack of consensus about how many different causes any one campaigner might espouse. This anticipated the many internal divisions the suffrage movement was to face over the final decades of the nineteenth century.

Chapter 1

Disappointment and defiance: the struggle during the late nineteenth century

In 1867, Millicent began working for what started as the Women's Suffrage Committee and came to be called the London Society for Women's Suffrage. The rest of the century was a time of great struggle but also great division in the suffrage movement. If Millicent thought the battle was to be straightforward, she was rapidly to be disabused.

The immediate response to Mill's petition was encouraging: 'For the first step forward had been taken, the challenge had been thrown down, and the Cause had been advanced into the political lists.'[1] This was extremely heartening to the fledgling suffrage societies formed not just in London but in Edinburgh and in Manchester, set up by the stalwart campaigner Lydia Becker in the case of Manchester. But they underestimated 'the formidable mass of hostility which really existed' and did not realise 'how preposterous and subversive their whole conception seemed, but continued to believe that because it was just it must be popular'.[2] It is from this period that the magazine *Punch* started its torrent of abusive cartoons against the suffragists and all who supported them. This represented the view not just of most cartoonists and politicians but of the vast majority of the general public.[3]

Even at this stage the various committees were grappling with issues of organisation and governance that were to concern the later, more mature

5. Punch cartoon, 'Militant suffragist', by Leo Cheney, 1913. Reproduced with permission of Punch Ltd., (www. punch.co.uk)

Fawcett Society and indeed almost every women's organisation of the nineteenth and twentieth centuries. Ray Strachey describes the challenges of decision-making (with committees that were either too large or too small and run entirely by volunteers, with all the tricky situations that brings) and all sorts of matters of policy[4] and the difficulties that societies all over the country had in co-operating with each other. A particularly thorny problem was Josephine Butler's highly contentious Contagious Diseases Act, felt by many to be not an appropriate subject for a respectable woman. This issue in effect split the women's movement.[5]

Towards the end of the 1860s a new tactic was developed – that of the public meeting. Speaking at such gatherings – which started with the genteel 'drawing room' meeting – took a lot of courage from women who had had little or no opportunity to speak in public before. As their confidence grew they would embark on speaking tours round the country. Millicent Fawcett in particular developed into a formidable, if never a particularly charismatic, speaker:

> Millicent Garrett Fawcett at the age of twenty-two set out on the first speaking tour of her sixty-year-long campaign for women's Suffrage. She would list the many reasons given as to why women should not be given the vote. It was said that women were intellectually inferior. They were physically inferior. They were too pure to be involved in politics. If given the vote, they would neglect their families and homes. Men would no longer open doors for them. Women did not really want the vote, and so on.
>
> Then, one by one, she would demolish these points using her sharp logical mind and quick wit. This powerful mix of reasoned arguments to promote a cause, combined with humour to keep the audience listening, remains a most effective strategy to this day.[6]

The fight for the suffrage was seen as part of a larger women's movement linked through participation in various campaigns, for instance on employment and the advancement of women in medicine. It was sometimes thought prudent to keep these campaigns separate – thus, Emily Davies along with Elizabeth Garrett had presented the 1866 petition to Parliament for women's enfranchisement to John Stuart Mill, but when she later concentrated her energies on girls' education she thought it wise to keep this movement separate from the suffrage campaign, 'to avoid the odium attaching to the claim for women's vote'. Similarly, Millicent Fawcett judged it better to dissociate the women's suffrage movement from Josephine Butler's campaign against the Contagious Diseases Act and the 'violent opposition which this aroused',[7] although she herself personally admired and supported Josephine Butler.

Although the present Fawcett Society's links with suffrage date from J. S. Mill's petition of 1866, campaigning for women's suffrage had started considerably earlier. Indeed, it could be argued that its roots go back to Mary Wollstonecraft and her *Vindication of the Rights of Woman* first published in 1792. In 1825, William Thompson, the Irish philosopher and social reformer, produced 'An appeal of one half of the human race, women, against the pretensions of the other half, men' to retain them in 'political, and thence in civil and domestic slavery'.[8] The passing of the Reform Bill in

1832 enfranchising 'male persons' only served to provide a focus of attack and a source of resentment from which in time the women's suffrage movement grew. The reference to 'adult male suffrage' in the People's Charter of 1838 led to women's political associations as part of the Chartist movement. At the same time, the incongruity had been noted between the fact that a woman was likely to inherit the throne (and did in 1837) but that no woman had the vote (although the same Queen would later express great hostility to women's suffrage).[9] Leaflets were published in 1843 (claiming equal rights with men) and 1847 (in favour of women's suffrage), an article on the 'The enfranchisement of women' appeared in 1851 by J. S. Mill's wife, Harriet, and a pamphlet in 1855 on 'The right of women to exercise the elective franchise' by Agnes Pochin.[10] Mass meetings were held in Birmingham and Shef-field in 1838 and 1851 respectively.

But the real action started in 1866 with the presentation by John Stuart Mill and Henry Fawcett to Parliament of a petition calling for enfranchisement without distinction of sex. (One of its signature slogans was the familiar 'no taxation without representation'.) Its emergence marked the beginning of a continuous struggle for women's suffrage, organised by women, extending until the vote was won.[11] The petition committee became the Provisional Committee in 1866 and in 1867 re-formed as the National Society for Obtaining Political Rights for Women, before being rapidly renamed the London National Society for Women's Suffrage, from which the Fawcett Society is directly descended. Meanwhile, societies in Manchester and Edinburgh, followed by Birmingham and Bristol, were all co-ordinated after 1872 by a Central Committee (the forerunner of the National Union of Women's Suffrage – NUWS – in 1897) and articles and discussions on the suffrage came too thick and fast to count. Lydia Becker showed herself an incomparable parliamentary campaigner. *The Women's Suffrage Journal*, whose first edition she edited in 1870, became an essential co-ordinating voice for the suffrage movement. Becker continued to edit the *Journal* until her death in July 1890 (when it folded, since it was unanimously agreed it could not continue without her).

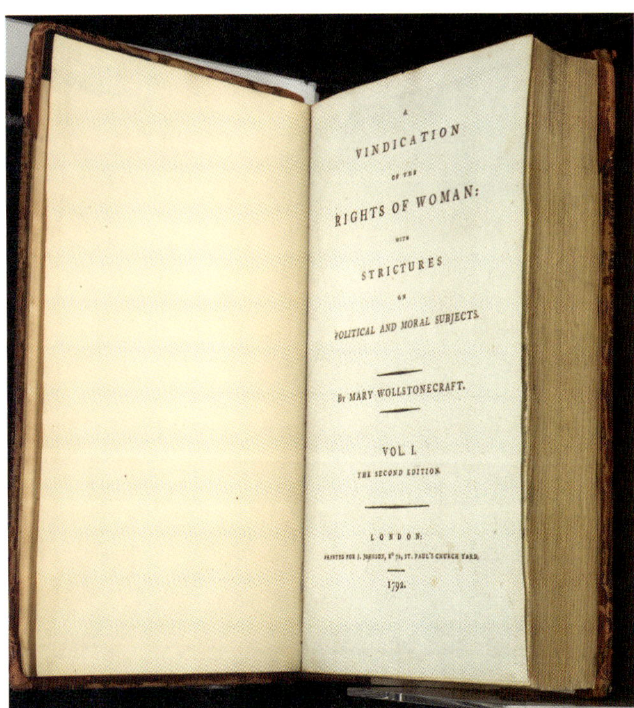

While the fight for the parliamentary vote was to prove extremely protracted and overwhelmingly disappointing, there was an early success in the attainment of the municipal franchise. The Municipal Corporation Act of 1869 was based on an occupational franchise and gave the vote

TO THE HONOURABLE THE COMMONS OF THE UNITED KINGDOM OF GREAT BRITAIN AND IRELAND IN PARLIAMENT ASSEMBLED.

The Humble Petition of the undersigned,

Sheweth,

That the exclusion of freeholders, householders, and ratepayers, legally qualified in every respect but that of sex, from the power of voting in the election of Members of your Honourable House, by depriving a considerable portion of the property, the industry, and the intelligence of the country of all direct representation, is injurious both to the persons excluded, and to the community at large.

That women are competent, both by law and in fact, to carry on a business, to administer an estate, and to fill other positions, which, both by investing them with interests requiring political representation, and by affording tests of fitness, are usually considered to give a claim to the suffrage.

That the admission of such persons to the privilege of the Franchise would be a measure in harmony with the principles of our representative system, while its beneficial effects would not be attended by any possibility of dangerous political consequences.

Your Petitioners therefore humbly pray that your Honourable House will take such measures as to your wisdom may seem fit for granting the suffrage to unmarried women and widows on the same conditions on which it is, or may be, granted to men.

And your Petitioners will ever pray.

NAME.   ADDRESS.

to women ratepayers, with the exception of married women[12] (although the Local Government Act of 1894 permitted duly qualified married women to vote). Women were furthermore allowed to serve on school boards from 1870, as Poor Law Guardians from 1875 and on Parish and District Councils after 1894. The question of voting rights for married women, alongside the issue of universal adult suffrage (since by no means did all men have the vote) and the issue of property qualifications, was to dog the debate for the parliamentary vote for the rest of the nineteenth century. The Married Women's Property Acts of 1870 to 1882 (on behalf of which a rigorous campaign was waged by, amongst others, Ursula Bright, wife of the suffragists' parliamentary supporter Jacob Bright MP) culminated in the act of 1882. 'The success of this measure of justice was tremendously encouraging to the agitators of the Women's Movement and it came at the time when their hopes of winning the suffrage were rising high.'[13] It also strengthened the arguments about property qualifications for the vote.

In 1869, Mill had published *The Subjection of Women*, considered of great help to the suffrage cause, but he also lost his parliamentary seat. However, the suffragists had great hopes of their new supporter, Jacob Bright, the Radical Liberal MP for Manchester, who in 1870 secured a day for the introduction of a Suffrage Bill. The Bill was drafted with care by Dr Richard Pankhurst, a Liberal lawyer from Manchester and great supporter of the suffrage cause (he was subsequently to marry Emmeline Goulden and become half of probably the most famous couple in the whole battle for the vote), and its second reading on 4 May was carried by 124 to 91. But it was then effectively killed by the determined opposition of the Liberal Prime Minister Mr Gladstone, with the

Opposite.
6. Mary Wollstonecraft, A Vindication of the Rights of Woman, *title page, 1792*

7. J.S. Mill's petition, 1866

8. NUWSS 'tree', cover of a NUWSS leaflet, 1913. At the foot is an acorn marked 1867, showing the date at which the first suffrage societies were started

voting reversed to 106 against. 'So ended the early hopes of parliamentary success. The women realised … the extent of the opposition they had to overcome.'[14] The organisation of the movement was meanwhile going through great turmoil. During 1871, the London Society made good progress in establishing Women's Suffrage Committees throughout the United Kingdom, with large meetings and the presentation of a considerable number of petitions. In the 1871 parliamentary session, the Women's Disabilities (Removal) Bill was again presented but lost 151 to 220. There was a feeling that all this increased activity called for a more centralised structure, which should nevertheless mean no loss of independence to individual committees. A great deal of debate and organisation was expended on setting up such a structure. The London Committee, however, was not prepared to accept the formation of the Central Committee and in the event the Central Committee of the National Society for Women's Suffrage was set up alongside the London Society for Women's Suffrage, which represented mainly London groups. J. S. Mill remained the president of the London Society until his death in 1873.

Jacob Bright lost his seat at the 1874 election, and his place as leader of the Suffrage Bill was taken first by Mr W. Forsyth, MP for Marylebone, and then by Leonard Courtney, MP for Bodmin. In 1877, Courtney not only took charge of the Bill but also attempted to heal the rift brought about by dissent over the Contagious Diseases Act. He brought together the two London-based societies under the name of the Central Committee for Women's Suffrage. With the schism set aside the Society pursued its goal with the same strategy and energy – continually raising petitions through its affiliates, bringing an annual measure before Parliament, holding local and national public meetings and producing a never-ceasing flow of leaflets and pamphlets.

A renewed split came in 1888, this time over an attempt to change the constitution, specifically the rules about admitting societies that were not fighting solely for the suffrage. These included, most significantly, those affiliated to the Liberal Party. Out of this debate came the re-formation of the movement on geographical lines, with the Central Committee becoming the Central and East of England Society, the Central National Society becoming the Central and Western Society, and the Manchester National Society becoming the North of England Society. Once again, however, the need for some centralised and concentrated effort of all suffrage committees became clear. This was partially met by the setting up of a Parliamentary Committee comprising a sub-committee from each Society to handle their activities among MPs. The renewed activity generated by this led directly in 1897 to the formation of the NUWSS – the National Union of Women's Suffrage Societies.

This move came out of a proposal at a special conference of all suffrage societies held in Birmingham in October 1896, to unite all district societies that made women's suffrage their sole object on a non-party basis. At the same time the two London-based societies, the Central and East of England and the Central and Western, amalgamated in 1900 as the Central Society for Women's Suffrage, with Mrs Fawcett as chair. Looking ahead to complete this picture of Fawcett's antecedents, we see the Central Society reverting to the name of the London Society for Women's Suffrage in 1907. This in turn became the London Society for Women's Service in 1919 (after the modi-

Figure 1: Evolution of the principal constitutional suffrage societies, late nineteenth to early twentieth centuries

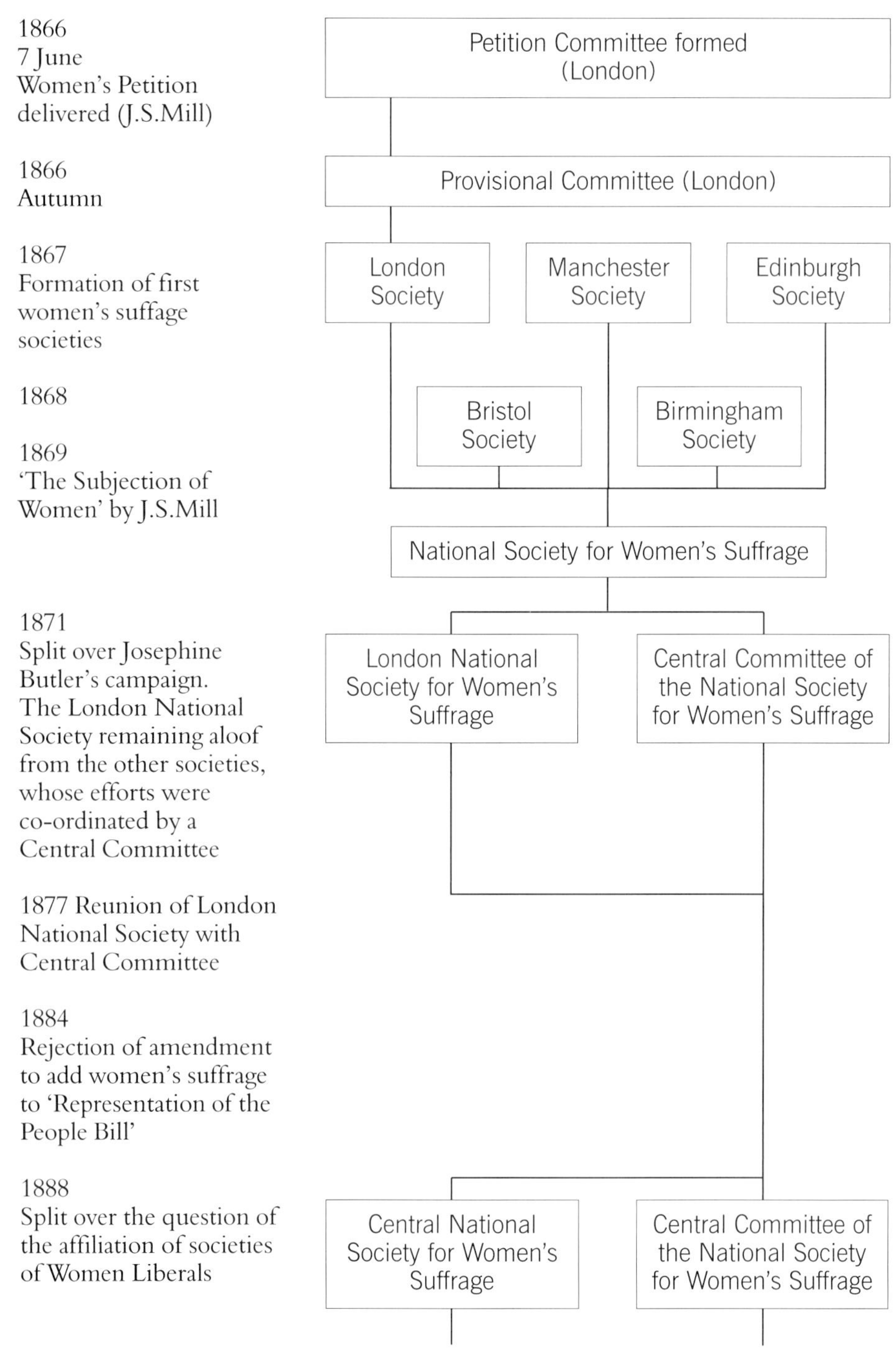

1897
Change of names and
division of spheres of
influence

1897
Union of all existing
societies organised
exclusively for women's
suffrage in a Federal
Society

1900
Reunion of the two
Central Societies (both
based in London), that
had kept apart even
though both were
members of the
NUWSS

1907
London Society lost its
co-ordinating function
and became simply a
Society of the National
Union

1914
First World War

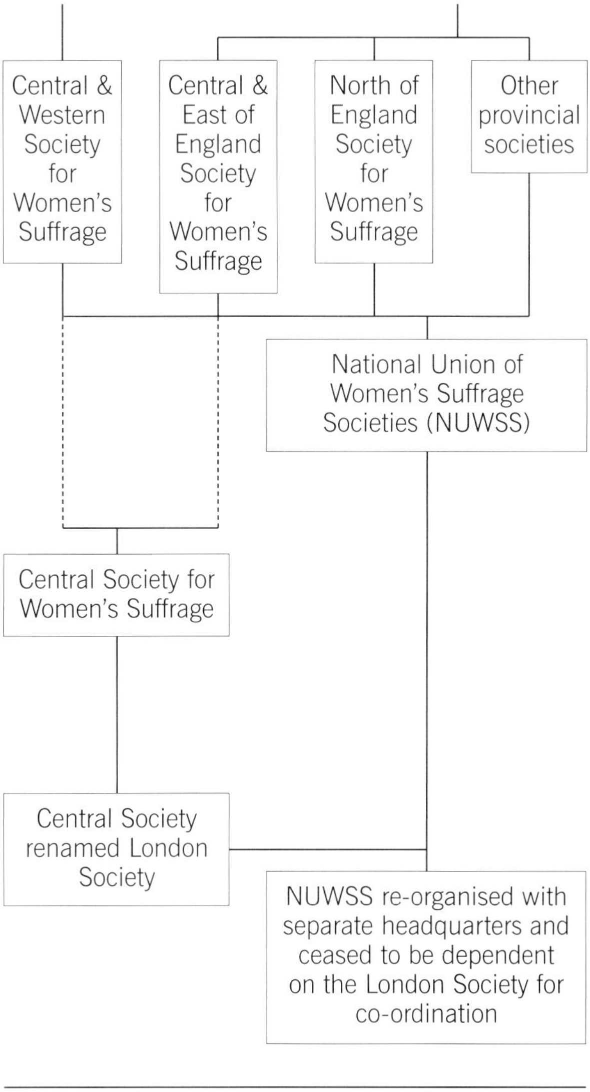

Adapted from Constance Rover, *Women's Suffrage and Party Politics in Britain 1866–1914*, pages 54/55

fied vote was achieved), the London and National Society for Women's Service in 1926 and finally the Fawcett Society itself in 1953.

The suffrage struggle was made up of many people, not only women: men like Mill, Bright, Pankhurst, Forsyth and Courtney were essential to the movement. But there were battalions of strong and resourceful women who were prepared to devote much of their lives to the fight for the suffrage – women such as Lydia Becker, Emily Davies, Frances Power Cobbe, Agnes and Rhoda Garrett, Margaret Pennington (the wife of Frederick Pennington MP), Miss Jessie Boucherett[15] and many, many more. Standing undoubtedly in the forefront of these battalions – serving over time on the board of most of the organisations, speaking on platforms all over the country, writing, lobbying – was Millicent Fawcett. Indeed, after the premature death of her husband Henry in 1884, Millicent devoted her time almost exclusively to the cause of the suffrage. In this she had something of a reputation for being very serious, even dour and a little forbidding. But she had a gentler, funnier side. In 1890, she was treasurer of the Central Committee of the National Society of Women's Suffrage and at its AGM on 15 July she drew parallels with the children's story of a king who had only three shillings and sixpence in his privy purse, and went on:

> My object in telling you this is to point out that my position as treasurer of this Society is far worse than that of the King in the play. He had three and sixpence: I have nothing: I have indeed less than nothing. I am a treasurer with nothing to treasure...our actual position is that we have about £22 less than nothing … I feel I have within me a capacity for treasuring which has never been called into activity. I could easily take care of quite a considerable sum of money and I appeal to you not to let my capacity for treasuring wither and die away for want of exercise...We let our moderation be known to all men: But it is a mistake to carry even such a good thing as moderation too far, it should not be carried into the subscription list.[16]

Millicent here is poking gentle fun at herself, but she also exposes how grindingly difficult it was to fund as well as run the suffrage movement – as indeed it has been to fund the women's movement ever since.

Things were not going well in Parliament either. Following the failure of Jacob Bright's Bill in 1870 and again in 1871, any further attempt by a private member to advance the cause of suffrage whether by Bill or by Resolution was greeted by a tone within the House that was 'not so much hostile as facetious'.[17] The next big opportunity came with the introduction of the Reform Bill of 1884 entitled the Representation of the People Bill. There had been an assumption amongst suffragists that the Liberals were the natural party of women's suffrage. In fact, while this might have been true of the rank and file it was not true of the leadership. It was Gladstone who virulently opposed William Woodall MP's women's suffrage amendment out of the fear he had 'lest we should invite her (woman) unwittingly to trespass upon the delicacy, the purity, the refinement, the elevation of her own nature which are the present sources of its power'.[18]

So the amendment failed to go through and suffragists, unconcerned about their purity, effectively lost faith in the Liberal Party Attempts by William Woodall to reintroduce his Bill failed, as did those by others. The nineteenth century drew to a close with an organisation for women's suffrage – the National Union of Women's Suffrage Societies – which at last seemed fit for purpose, but with virtually no progress towards the goal of votes for women. Yet these women also showed remarkable resilience. After more than forty years of struggle they had achieved very little. They were having to send letters of congratulations to places like Australia and Wyoming, which had achieved what they had so spectacularly failed to win. And yet again and again their minute books end with the assurance that although things have gone badly so far, they are sure to go better in the coming year. It was to take a new century for this to become true.

THE FIGHT FOR EDUCATION

We saw in the Introduction how Emily Davies as a young woman dedicated herself to bringing higher education to women. But before higher education there was a need for secondary education for girls. In the mid-nineteenth century the choice was generally between an inadequate 'dame' school or an unqualified governess at home – or nothing at all. (Millicent Garrett was very fortunate to have, unusually, received a reasonable education at Miss Browning's school in Blackheath.)

The struggle for secondary education was led by the indefatigable Miss Dorothea Beale along with Miss Frances Buss ('how different from us').[1] Between them they established or developed respectively Cheltenham Ladies' College (from 1858) and the rather less elitist North London Collegiate and Camden School for Girls. They threw themselves into the 'task of forcing up the standard of girls' schools, and did not flinch before the lack of teachers, the lack of funds, the doubting parents, the hostile Press, or the hampering and clogging atmosphere of public ridicule.'[2] The all-age Queen's College for Women had already been established in 1848 and Bedford College in 1849. Yet more schools were inspired by Cheltenham Ladies College, such as Roedean, Wycombe Abbey and Downe House. The Girls' Public Day School Trust was set up in 1872 to co-ordinate and support these independent high schools. All these establishments catered for the middle and upper classes; working-class girls had to make do with less.

If Beale and Buss were the champions of secondary education, then Emily Davies was undoubtedly that of higher education for women. But there were some preliminary steps needed before she could make a full frontal attack on the universities. In 1862, she became the secretary and mainspring of a committee to secure the admission of women to examinations that would allow them to qualify for admission to universities (in which it was eventually successful) and her tactful but determined approach led in 1868 to a Report by the Schools Enquiry Commission which pointed to inadequately trained teachers and lack of funding as problems especially affecting girls' education. These were the essential first steps.

There was, however, little point in being allowed to take the qualifying exams if no university would admit a female. So in 1869 Emily set about establishing her own university college in microcosm in the village of Hitchin with herself and five other young women and a great deal of support from Elizabeth Garrett Anderson, Barbara Bodichon and other members of the Langham Place Ladies. By the time this precursor of Girton College was able to move to its new building in Cambridge in 1873 there were fifteen students. This was followed by Newnham College in Cambridge (developed by Henry Sidgwick and Anne Clough, 1874), Somerville and Lady Margaret

Hall (1879) and St Hilda's College (1893) in Oxford. The watershed date was 1878 when women were first admitted on equal terms with men at the University of London. Thereafter, all six universities founded before the First World War in England, with those in Wales and Ireland, provided in their Charters for the acceptance of women on equal terms with men, while the more ancient universities all over the British Isles dragged their feet.[3]

But just getting to university did not mean as a young woman you were in for a smooth ride. Jane Robinson's book *Bluestockings* and Jessica Swale's play of the same name[4] testify to the atrocious misogyny, hostility, ridicule and even invisibility which these pioneering women faced. Probably most damaging was the work of the psychiatrist Dr Henry Maudsley, who believed fervently in the concept of the 'wandering womb' and that women's brains were on average five ounces lighter than men's:

> It is not that girls have not ambition, nor that they fail generally to run the intellectual race which is set before them, but it is asserted that they do it at a cost to their strength and health which entails lifelong suffering, and even incapacitates them for the adequate performance of the natural functions of their sex … For it would be an ill thing, if it should so happen, that we got the advantages of a quantity of female intellectual work at the price of a puny, enfeebled and sickly race.[5]

Things improved immeasurably, but while women could graduate from elsewhere, starting with the University of London, at Oxford and Cambridge women could take the final exams but could not receive a degree. This was to be achieved for Oxford in 1920 but, in spite of a protest in Cambridge over degrees for women in 1897, it took a further half-century – till 1948 – for Cambridge to give degrees to its women students, thus making it an even longer struggle than that for the vote.

There are many, many links between the two campaigns – for the suffrage and for education – but perhaps the most symbolic was made by Philippa, the daughter of Millicent and Henry Fawcett:

> There was no one who might hold to be so truly a product of the Women's Movement, no one who was more fully representative of the new generation and her success or failure were thus of particular importance.[6]

In 1890, Philippa was to receive the extreme accolade from Cambridge, being placed in her Mathematical Tripos 'above the senior wrangler', thus winning one of the most famous mathematical honours in the world. No one again could ever claim women were not fit for higher education, or for the vote for that matter.[7]

Chapter 2

Into militancy: relationships with the WSPU and the suffragette movement

The nineteenth century ended with Millicent Fawcett as president of the National Union of Women's Suffrage Societies (NUWSS), formalised in 1897 (although with its origins in 1867) but with progress towards the goal of votes for women virtually non-existent. For thirty-five years Mrs Fawcett's suffragists had shown themselves determined, stoic and resolutely non-violent, but in spite of an enormous network of local suffrage groups, numbering in the hundreds and clustered under different regional bodies, any progress towards votes for women was almost imperceptible and had in fact been stopped in its tracks by the action, or rather inaction, of political parties, all of which proved inadequate in their response. The Conservatives tended to follow the pattern of a leadership that favoured a limited form of women's suffrage, while the rank and file opposed it. For the Liberals it tended to be the other way round. Asquith, who became prime minister in 1908, had 'never concealed his dislike of the cause'[1] and both he and other Liberal leaders – Gladstone, Rosebery, Campbell-Bannerman, Churchill, even Lloyd George – remained somewhat ambivalent in their support. The most hopeful source of political support seemed to be the Independent Labour Party (ILP; first formed as a national party in 1893), whose leader Keir Hardie, the Ayrshire Miners' Secretary, remained a supporter of the women's cause all his life. The ILP was in due course to become part of the evolving Labour Party.

It was to the tangled relationships between the ILP, the trade union movement, the Women's Cooperative Guild and the radical suffragists[2] of the Lancashire cotton mills (led by such women as Eva Gore-Booth, Esther Roper, Sarah Reddish, Sarah Dickenson, Selina Cooper and Ada Nield Chew) that the Women's Social and Political Union (WSPU) owed its origins. It was in Manchester, home of one of the earliest suffrage groups started by Lydia Becker nearly forty years earlier, that the WSPU was born. The Pankhursts – Richard, Emmeline and their four children – had lived in Manchester since 1894. Richard, in particular, 'champion of all progressive causes',[3] had a long involvement with the suffrage struggle there. Richard died suddenly in 1898. Emmeline had till then shown very little interest in the suffrage, devoting most of her energies to the ILP. After the shock of Richard's death, Emmeline took no part in any feminist activity for three years, although she and Richard had previously helped to set up the Women's Franchise League. This was an organisation which aimed to extend female enfranchisement beyond what many saw as the obsession of traditional suffrage organisations with giving the vote only to 'widows and spinsters' (i.e. women who owned property). From 1901 to 1904, however, Emmeline's daughter Christabel had been working with Esther Roper and Eva Gore-Booth in the North of England Society for Women's Suffrage. An interest in Christabel's work, coupled with the mounting unemployment and short-time employment of women cotton operatives, led Emmeline to talk of 'the need for a new organization which would fight for the interests of working class women',[4] in whom even the ILP seemed to take very little interest. The WSPU was born, quietly and without fanfare, during the autumn of 1903.

For the first few months the WSPU attracted very little attention and was very low key in its operation. Meetings were mostly held at the Pankhursts' Manchester home at 62 Nelson Street, organisation was very loose and no minutes or accounts appear to have been kept. But in December 1903 it published, in an attention-grabbing bright yellow pamphlet, its suffrage resolution, which stated:

> That for all purposes connected with, and having reference to, the right to vote at Parliamentary elections, words in the Representation of the People Act importing the masculine gender shall include women.

This was much the same demand Richard Pankhurst had made in 1869. Emmeline now lobbied candidates from the ILP and the fledgling Labour coalition but, realising that power lay elsewhere, Christabel on 4 February 1904 took the message to the Free Trade Hall in Manchester, where she interrupted Winston Churchill's speech on free trade, asking that the Representation of the People's Acts be amended so that words expressed in the masculine gender would be construed to include women. This was good publicity (indeed WSPU's first militant step) but it clearly did not lead to women's suffrage; nor did the Private Member's Women's Enfranchisement Bill, which was 'talked out' when it got to a second reading in the House of Commons on 12 May 1905.

At this stage WSPU tactics were not that much different from those of the NUWSS, who were perfecting the traditional middle-class methods of organising public meetings, demonstrating, writing propaganda literature, raising money, lobbying MPs and petitioning Parliament. The NUWSS, governed by an executive committee composed of distinguished representatives of the member societies, led by Millicent Fawcett, strove for full democratic accountability and increasingly for more control over member organisations and their activism in the constituencies. The Liberal Election victory in 1906 did not, unfortunately, lead to any measure of women's suffrage

In its early days WSPU's main activities were public meetings, mainly outdoor, all over the north of England. Its list of speakers rose to six with Annie Kenney, Teresa Billington and Hannah Mitchell added to the three Pankhurst daughters – Christabel, Sylvia and Adela. However, frustrated by the lack of any sort of government response,

Christabel planned a more militant event. Returning to the Free Trade Hall on 13 October 1905 with Annie Kenney and a banner reading 'Votes for Women', she attempted to ask a question, 'Will the Liberal Government give women the vote?', of the speaker, the Liberal politician Sir Edward Grey. When this failed to get a response, they created a disturbance and were removed from the hall, hitting out (and spitting) at the police. Subsequently accused of disorderly behaviour and refusing to pay a fine, they were imprisoned for between three and seven days, with large demonstrations at the prison gates on their release.

This was a quite deliberate tactic. 'Martyrdom deliberately sought after, would make women's suffrage *newsworthy*',[5] and Christabel's calculations proved correct. Militancy *was* news. The incident was widely covered in the press. Attendance at WSPU meetings rose and membership grew. Andrew Rosen has pointed to the basic pattern in militant feminist campaigning: 'pre-planned militant tactics led to imprisonment and, thus, martyrdom, which led to newspaper coverage (i.e. free publicity) which led in turn to increased membership and funds for the WSPU'.[6] Meanwhile, the constitutional suffragists of the NUWSS continued to maintain that 'moral force was a more effective, and a more honourable, weapon than physical force, and they feared that once the use of violence was countenanced, it would be impossible to put an end to it'.[7] But undoubtedly the increased activism of the WSPU inspired more frenetic NUWSS activity – a new constitution in 1907, new premises and preparations to introduce a women's suffrage bill into Parliament.

Disturbances at public meetings by the WSPU continued, including, spectacularly, a meeting with Campbell-Bannerman at the Albert Hall on 21 December 1905. But essentially until January 1906 the WSPU was still a tiny provincial movement, substantially funded by the ILP, which had only intervened in the General Election in the north. The Liberal Party's victory of 1906 finally pushed the WSPU towards moving out of 'the somewhat parochial world of Northern Labour politics'.[8]

This move on London was led by Sylvia Pankhurst and Annie Kenney, who in February 1906 hired (with financial help from Keir Hardie) – and filled – the Caxton Hall in Westminster for a meeting mainly of women from the East End of London, who subsequently marched on Parliament to demand of the Liberal government why there was nothing in the King's speech on votes for women. The publicity from this brought in many new members, including Emmeline and Frederick Pethick-Lawrence, who brought not only fervour for the cause but money and organisational skills. Mrs Pethick-Lawrence was soon made the WSPU's treasurer and began to bring some order to their chaotic finances. (This position was later taken by her husband.) A failed attempt to take thirty women to 10 Downing Street on 9 March to speak to Campbell-Bannerman meant that the recently coined word 'suffragette' began to come into general use, starting with the front page of the *Daily Mail*. Further activities followed, led by confrontations with Liberal politicians. These resulted in October 1906 in the arrest in the House of Commons of ten women (many of them distinguished, including Mrs Anne Cobden Sanderson). All were found guilty of 'using threatening and abusive words and behaviour with intent to provoke a breach of the peace' and, when sentenced, chose imprisonment, even though this meant two months in the

Second Division, i.e. being treated as common criminals. This sentence was later changed to the First Division after great protest.

These events again brought a huge response in terms of funds donated to WSPU, new members and positive press coverage. But the WSPU was changing. It no longer pretended to be an organisation overwhelmingly of 'working women'. This switch in emphasis very much helped it grow as women of all political sympathies and social class were made equally welcome. It could also more easily attract wealthy donors. The emphasis on 'Votes for women ' became an end in itself. At the same time, the organisation was becoming more formalised (their first Annual Report was published in 1907), although any attempts at democratisation were put in reverse by 'the Split' of 1907 when Mrs Pankhurst, Christabel and the Pethick-Lawrences in effect took entire control, with the WSPU run on almost military lines. *Votes for Women* became its mouthpiece in October. Most of the women who had joined from the Labour movement now left and the WSPU became increasingly polarised into leaders and led. A consequence of this was the formation of the breakaway Women's Freedom League (WFL), led by Charlotte Despard and Anne Cobden Sanderson, who wished to see an organisation run on democratic, non-violent lines. The WFL was to play a considerable role in the subsequent fight for the suffrage and remained in existence until 1961. In 1909 its philosophy of 'political passive resistance' led to the setting-up of a sister organisation, the Tax Resistance League ('No taxation without representation') and in 1911 it was very prominent in the campaign against the census ('No vote. No census').

1906-07 saw hugely increased activity, constant onslaughts on Parliament and many arrests. Dinners or breakfasts to welcome women as they came out of prison were instituted, having the double function of also bringing marvellous publicity. Increased funding meant Mrs Pankhurst and Christabel could now resign from the ILP, on which the WSPU had been so dependent in the early days. Increased activity by the suffragists followed in 1907, with mass meetings and processions including the notorious Mud March of 7 February and the beginning of their new tactic of involvement in by-elections. On 13 February 1908, Mrs Pankhurst was arrested and imprisoned for the first time when she marched to Parliament with twelve other women following the Women's Parliament in Caxton Hall.[9]

At this stage Mrs Fawcett and the suffragists were generally supportive of the militants, seeing them as giving an added propaganda boost to the suffragist cause. Initially their response was to give a dinner for women coming out of prison, and in 1905 Mrs Fawcett made public her support of the Free Trade Hall incident. In 1906 Mrs Fawcett wrote to the *Times* to support the suffragettes. She visited her friend Anne Cobden Sanderson in prison and later held a testimonial banquet at the Savoy Hotel in honour of recently released prisoners. It was not till 1908, when Asquith became prime minister and the WSPU intensified militancy with window-breaking, stone-throwing and arson (although never intended to endanger life), that even the conciliatory Mrs Fawcett and the NUWSS began to condemn the violence.

For the WSPU, increased activity demanded more sophisticated fund-raising. Famous authors like John Galsworthy gave signed copies of their books, and Mrs Pethick-Lawrence urged WSPU members to have a 'self-denial' week by doing with-

9. Flora
Drummond,
Emmeline and
Christabel
Pankhurst under
arrest, 13 October
1908

out luxuries. On 19 March 1908, at a massive meeting of 7,000 at the Albert Hall, it was announced that £7,000 had been raised. The next big event was a huge meeting in Hyde Park on 21 June, designed to prove to the government that there really was a national demand for women's enfranchisement. It was claimed 'that the number of people present was the largest ever gathered together on one spot at one time in the history of the world' (*Votes for Women*, 25 June 1908). Even the *Daily Chronicle* (22 June) estimated numbers as over 300,000. This ambitious gathering, organised by Mrs Flora Drummond (a.k.a. 'General' Drummond because of the military-style uniform she wore at the front of WSPU processions), was fed by seven processions from all over London carrying 700 banners, and had twenty platforms with different speakers throughout the park. It was the first time Mrs Pethick-Lawrence's WSPU colours – purple, white and green – were on display (purple for dignity, white for purity in public as well as private life, green for hope). These colours were also used to the full in extensive merchandising of WSPU memorabilia (scarves, sashes, badges, jewellery, tea sets, games and so forth, many using designs created by Sylvia Pankhurst), which became an important means of fund-raising (See Box on suffrage colours).

Unfortunately Asquith did not respond positively to the resolution passed in Hyde Park 'that this meeting calls upon the Government to grant votes to women without delay', and Christabel vowed a return to militancy. Stones were thrown in Downing Street.

> Frustration at the failure of both large peaceful demonstrations and mild forms of militancy alike to achieve tangible progress towards women's enfranchisement, when that frustration was exacerbated by brutal treatment at the hands of men, had set off resentment strong enough to lead to acts of militancy beyond the pale of existing WSPU policy.[10]

When Edith New and Mary Leigh were released from Holloway in August 1908, they were greeted with a brass band and their landau was drawn by a team of suffragettes. This was to become the norm, deliberately so since, as Mrs Pethick-Lawrence remarked, 'every prisoner means a harvest of converts' (*Daily News*, 2 July). A well-publicised plan 'to rush the House of Commons' in October led to the arrest of Mrs Pankhurst, Christabel and Mrs Drummond for distributing handbills. The WSPU continued to heckle government ministers very effectively at every opportunity. In the Albert Hall in December, Lloyd George took two hours to complete what should have been a twenty-minute speech.

The start of militancy

The WSPU's Third Annual Report in March 1910 revealed a hugely expanded organisation – in funds, membership, attendance at events (including weekly 'At Homes'), staff and premises both in London and around the country, and in the circulation of *Votes for Women*. (By February 1909 the newsheet had become a twenty-four-page weekly with a circulation of 16,000.) A uniformed women's fife and drum band had been formed. The movement's tactics, however, had changed very little and virtually no headway had been made with the Liberal government. The WSPU might have succeeded in making women's suffrage 'a heatedly debated issue', but showed little 'tangible progress towards persuading the Government to sponsor women's suffrage legislation'.[11]

Now was the time for change and the beginning of violence. A small delegation to Parliament led by Mrs Pankhurst in June 1909 resulted in a melee and many arrests. This was followed by window-breaking down Whitehall. The convicted window-breakers ultimately chose prison rather than fines, refused to accept being put in the Second Division and, after six days on hunger strike, were released. Hunger strikes became a recognised form of resistance. Attacks on Liberal politicians grew. In autumn 1909 the notorious force-feeding began to be used for WSPU hunger-strikers in prison. Descriptions of this process are appalling, whether it took place via the throat or nostrils – it was painful, brutal and dangerous. WSPU condemned it as a horrible outrage and torture, although they were equally aware that its very severity helped to attract support. Lady Constance Lytton's successful attempt to pass as a working-class woman, Jane Warton, reinforced the belief that working-class women were treated particularly badly in prison. Elsie Duval's prison diary of 1913 gives a graphic and appalling description of what it was like to be on the receiving end of this particular form of treatment, an experience both excruciatingly painful and humiliating.[12]

Herbert Gladstone, the Home Secretary, felt decidedly hunted. In a letter of 9 November 1909 he wrote with some exasperation:

> But for three years I have been pursued by the militant section with venom & falsehood simply because I have been discharging a public duty. These persons choose to organize disturbances and to commit assaults … They refuse to find sureties for good behaviour, & to pay fines. They elect to go to prison. They elect to refuse food. They elect to resist Forcible feeding. They demand to be released after 2 or 3 days in order to create fresh disturbances. They wish to have it all ways…[13]

Mrs Fawcett and the suffragists were also beginning to feel considerable frustration. Relations between the NUWSS and the WSPU had been to date fairly cordial, but with the violence came the perception that the militants 'were no longer martyrs but criminals', whose methods 'threatened to create anarchy, and would certainly destroy any chance for the enactment of a women's suffrage measure'.[14] The same applied to relationships with Parliament and the wider public:

> Militancy … had begun to exert an adverse effect on the fortunes of the suffrage movement. Whereas in 1906 the actions of the WSPU had abetted the cause of women's suffrage, by 1909 the increasingly violent behavior of the suffragettes had begun to alienate many former supporters, particularly in Parliament.[15]

It was the election of January 1910, when the Liberals lost an overall majority in the Commons, that opened the door to some movement. Faced with the new reality, the radical journalist H. N. Brailsford began to talk of founding a new committee that would promote a new Suffrage Bill. He wrote to Mrs Fawcett on 18 January 1910:

> I have some thought of attempting to found a Conciliation Committee for Women's Suffrage. My idea is that it should undertake the necessary diplomatic work of promoting an early settlement. It should not be large, and should consist of both men and women – the women in touch with the existing societies but not their more prominent leaders, the men also as far as possible not identified officially with either party…[16]

This led Mrs Pankhurst to declare a truce of all militant tactics, which were suspended until November 1911. WSPU had by then expanded enormously both at headquarters in London (with ninety-eight staff) and twenty-six salaried organisers around the country.

In parliamentary terms, the only hope for suffragists and suffragettes alike was the Conciliation Bill. This was very narrow, based on a property qualification which only affected about one million women. But its very narrowness gave its supporters, including Christabel, hope. However, once more Asquith killed the Bill, ensuring it got no further than a second reading. During the summer and autumn of 1910, WSPU held

10. Board game, *Suffragettes In and Out of Prison*.

large meetings both in London and around the country. When Parliament resumed in November with no mention of the Conciliation Bill, a deputation of 300 women converged on the Commons on 18 November to be met with extreme police brutality, including sexual violence. This came to be known as Black Friday, and was substantially blamed, seemingly erroneously, on Churchill, the new home secretary. 'The battle of Downing Street' in November resulted in an injury to the knee of Augustine Birrell, the chief secretary for Ireland. The first half of 1911 seemed to bring more hope for the Conciliation Bill, but by the autumn it was clear that the Liberal government was once more blocking it, instead proposing a Manhood Suffrage Bill.

During the period of truce throughout most of 1911, the campaign against the census, led by the WSPU and the WFL and largely influenced by the Women's Tax Resistance League (WTRL), reached its culmination. This was a problematic campaign because for its part the government 'sold' the census as a way of supporting Lloyd George's National Insurance Bill (asking such sensitive questions as the number of dead babies within a marriage), with those refusing to comply seen as committing a 'crime against science'. The suffragettes meanwhile saw their demand for women's citizenship, for representation in exchange for information, as the crucial political priority. This meant that the support for census evasion and resistance (which was the form the campaign took) while passionate and enthusiastic, was not universal. Most suffragists, for instance, did not support it, and Philippa Strachey of the London Society for Women's Suffrage (LSWS) entirely supported the NUWSS decision against the boycott.

In the event the census went ahead on 2 April with some spectacular evasions (Emily Wilding Davison hiding in a cupboard in the House of Commons, the mass skating at the Aldwych, women with large houses throwing open their homes to mass evasions, with women sleeping in rows on the floor) but little effect on the overall outcome and, in the event, no prosecutions for evaders or resisters. On 17 June, WSPU, WFL (with their new 'Census protest banner'), NUWSS and LSWS came together for the Women's Coronation Procession, in which 'forty thousand women marched together, constitutionalists and militants alike, joined in a spirit of optimistic and determined co-operation'.[17]

Despite this show of harmony, as far as the WSPU was concerned, the 'era of conciliation' came to an end with mass window-breaking on 21 November 1911. This was followed by Emily Wilding Davison's setting fire to post-boxes (not official WSPU policy) and in February 1912 by an onslaught on plate glass windows all over London (this was official WSPU policy). Such action put Mrs Pankhurst and the Pethick-Lawrences into prison – although Christabel managed to escape to Paris – and resulted in a very hostile reaction from both the press and politicians who had until then been sympathetic – and indeed the general public. This was accompanied by increasing disenchantment with the militants on the part of Mrs Fawcett, as her correspondence with Lloyd George late in 1911 makes clear.

On 30 November 1911, Lloyd George wrote to her, seemingly in response to a letter she had sent him:

11. Arrest of a suffragette, Black Friday, 18 November 1910

My dear Mrs Fawcett,

I thank you for your appreciative note, which I value very much coming from you. I have been very unhappy about the prospects during the last few days. The action of the Militants is alienating sympathy from the women's cause in every quarter: I felt the depressing influence even at the meeting at Bath. Tuesday's violence and last night's indecent exhibition, when the Prime Minister supporting a charitable institution was howled down in a place of worship, have between them created a very grave situation. If next year's chances of carrying either a women's amendment or a Bill are not to be totally ruined, some emphatic action must be taken at once. You can hardly realise what the feeling is even amongst members of Parliament who have hitherto been steadfast in their support of Women's Suffrage … What do you suggest? Anti-Suffragists are of course exultant. I feel confident that the effect of our agitation will be neutralised by the antics of the Militants.

To which Mrs Fawcett replied on 2 December 1911:

My dear Mr Lloyd George,

I regret and deplore, condemn also, if the word must be used, the disgusting scenes of November 21st and 29th as much as you do. The National Union has always condemned methods of violence. My Suffrage friends are constantly asking me, can nothing be done to stop them? In my opinion, nothing can be done by direct or indirect appeal to the leaders of the Women's Social and Political Union. That has been tried again and again on other occasions by other Suffragists, and always without result.

I entreat you and Sir Edward Grey, and other Suffragists in the Cabinet to approach the whole subject in the spirit in which Lord Morley and the Cabinet approached the subject of the recent unrest in India. That unrest was manifested by a series of terrible crimes, compared with which breaking windows and preventing the Prime Minister from delivering a speech (disagreeable and offensive as they are) sink into insignificance.[18]

Her letter went on to take up Lord Morley's argument that unrest in India would be best countered by tackling the root causes of discontent, to make the point that suffragette excesses would also be best dealt with by addressing the basic grievance.

Mrs Pankhurst and the Pethick-Lawrences were sentenced in May 1912 and joined forty-five other hunger strikers in prison. On their release divisions emerged in the senior leadership of the party, mainly over militancy, and the Pethick-Lawrences agreed to leave, since they did not wish to split the party as a whole, however personally betrayed they might feel. Their departure was announced at a large Albert Hall meeting in October at which Mrs Pankhurst gave a passionate address, and was reported both in *Votes for Women*, edited by Frederick Pethick-Lawrence, and in *The Suffragette*, the official organ of the WSPU edited by Christabel. The Pethick-Lawrences' departure had a big influence on the organisational structure of the WSPU, to which they had contributed enormously, although its effect on policy is less clear.

The loss of the Conciliation Bill brought recriminations on all sides. Brailsford was angry with Lloyd George for 'striking a "strident party note" by jubilantly declaring that he had "torpedoed" the supposedly Tory-inspired Conciliation Bill, but he was quite as

12. Daily Herald *cartoon, 'The New Advocate', by Will Dyson, 1913, marking Emily Davison's death*

angry with the militants for using methods that were both futile and bankrupt … The NUWSS was just as furious…', and Mrs Fawcett issued a manifesto denouncing the actions of the militants.[19] Suffragist disappointment with the Liberals was solidified and pushed them closer to an alliance with the Labour Party.

While Christabel was guiding the WSPU from the centre, her sister Sylvia,[20] a trained artist, socialist and champion of the rights of working women, was mounting a suffrage campaign from the periphery, with working-class women in the East End. This was centred on the re-election of George Lansbury, the Labour MP for Bromley and Bow and a great supporter of the WSPU. In the event Lansbury was defeated in November 1912. The shock of this released WSPU tactics that were for the first time oblivious to public opinion. The first of these was letter-destroying, where letters were destroyed in their letter-boxes all over the country. This was not at all a popular move, but the WSPU now felt conventional, legal tactics such as speeches, demonstrations and canvassing were completely futile. Instead of being asking for their support, the public was to be forced into asking the government to grant women the vote.

The WSPU postponed its concerted campaign of destruction of private and public property when asked by NUWSS to see what would happen to the women's suffrage amendments to the Franchise and Registration Bill of 1913, on which NUWSS placed great hopes. When these failed, WSPU slipped further into the mind-set of seeing all cabinet ministers as the 'enemy'. Led by Mrs Pankhurst, WSPU followers declared themselves on a war footing, with suffragettes as 'guerrillists' who would do as much damage to property as they could and, at the end of January 1913, a concerted campaign of destruction began. Mrs Pankhurst accepted full responsibility, fully realising how unpopular this action was:

> We are not destroying Orchid Houses, breaking windows, cutting telegraph wires, injuring golf greens, in order to win the approval of the people who were attacked. If the general public were pleased with what we are doing, that would be a proof that our war is ineffective. We don't intend you should be pleased.[21]

Such actions evoked enormous hostility from both the press and the general public. WSPU members were subjected to physical attack and their activities curtailed. Mrs Pankhurst was sentenced to three years in prison. In April 1913, the Prisoners' Temporary Discharge for Ill-Health Act was brought in, soon to be known as the 'Cat and Mouse Act', whereby prisoners who damaged their health through their own conduct, e.g. by hunger strikes, could be temporarily released to recover, and then be re-imprisoned. This removed the necessity for forced feeding. Mrs Pankhurst was subjected to this process a number of times. Militancy – and damage to property – continued, with increasingly drastic penalties served on the newspaper *The Suffragette* and other manifestations of WSPU infrastructure and staff. For the WSPU the struggle was increasingly seen in terms of good and evil, light and darkness. A growing concern with sexual morality (including the white slave trade) heightened this mood, with winning the vote seen as a triumph of moral righteousness.

Among the organisation's most extreme actions was Emily Wilding Davison's deci-

sion to disrupt the Derby at Epsom on 4 June 1913. Davison, one of the WSPU's most militant but erratic members, went to the race with a return ticket in her purse and WSPU banners concealed in her coat and died under the hooves of the King's horse Anmer. There has been intense speculation both then and ever since as to whether this was suicide or a protest that went wrong. But although it is doubtful whether Emily's death actually hastened votes for women, she certainly became one of the most – if not *the* most – iconic and emblematic figures of the suffragette movement. At her funeral in London her coffin, draped in purple, white and green, was escorted by 2,000 suffragettes through streets lined with miles of spectators. And the centenary of her death in 2013 was marked by events and exhibitions all over the country, culminating with a memorial in Westminster Hall attended by 800 women and addressed by parliamentarians of all parties.

In 1913 the campaign of arson intensified. Membership of WSPU was falling and schisms were appearing in the party. For a start it was obvious that Christabel did not approve of her sister Sylvia, who had been rebuilding the East London Federation of the WSPU as a semi-autonomous group which advocated universal adult suffrage, had a working-class membership, was not anti-male and did not sponsor arson. In May 1914, Mary Richardson slashed Velasquez's *Rokeby Venus* at the National Gallery in protest against Mrs Pankhurst's arrest in Glasgow. This was followed by a rash of

13. Women heading to London in one of the 'pilgrims' marches', 1913

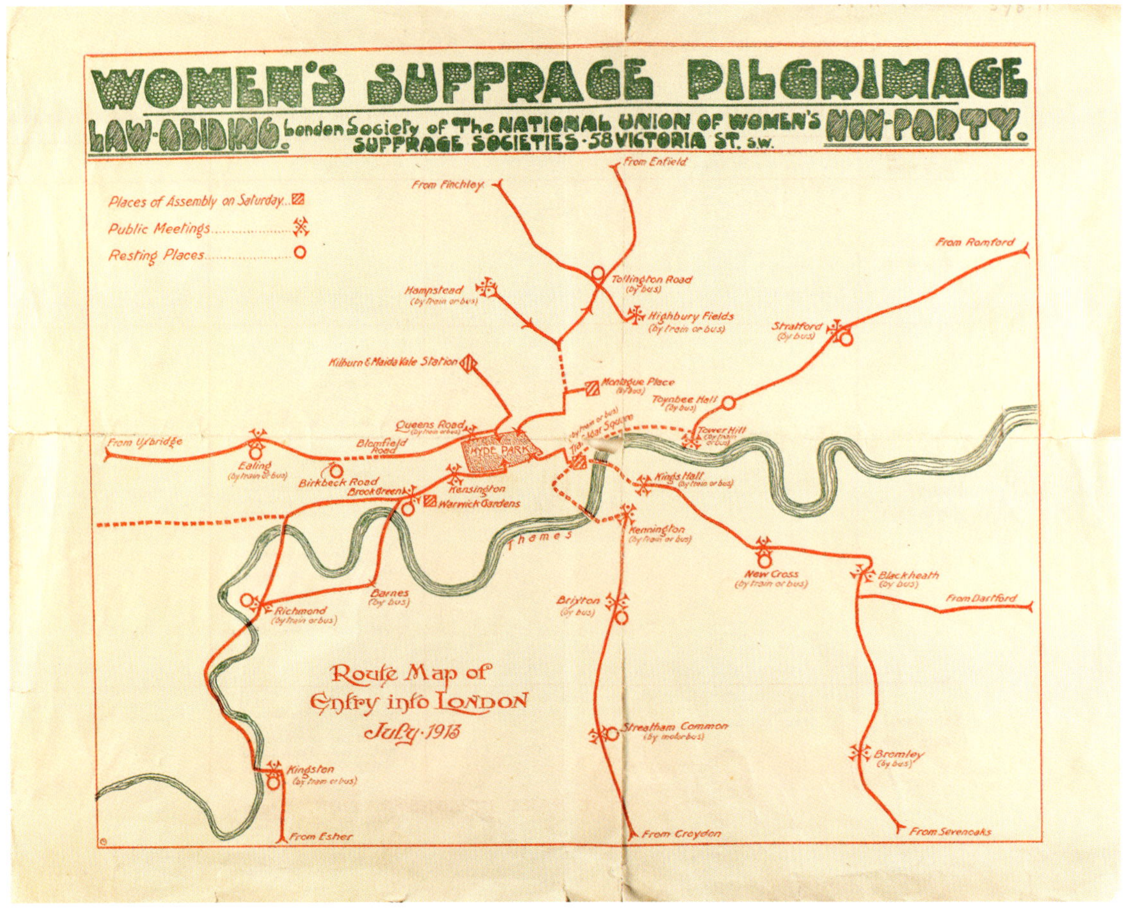

14. Map of the women's suffrage pilgrimage routes into London, 1913

attacks against art objects. Approaches to Liberal politicians, and indeed to George V, proved abortive. WSPU premises were raided and distribution of *The Suffragette* threatened, so that the organisation was forced to go partially underground. It was rapidly losing support with the public. Mrs Pankhurst and others were sick from repeated hunger strikes but the arson attacks continued.

NUWSS tactics

The NUWSS response, on the other hand, was one of intense negotiation. They fought for two years for the Conciliation Bill, writing letters, organising deputations, courting politicians and devising countless other lobbying strategies. They sponsored a meeting in the Albert Hall on 23 February 1912 which the *Manchester Guardian* of 24 February termed 'probably the most impressive held in London'.[22] Once it was clear all was lost, and in spite of intense disappointment, they turned their attentions and hopes to the women's suffrage amendment to the Franchise and Registration Bill and to setting up an election fighting fund (EFF) which would help elect Labour members of Parliament against Liberal anti-suffragists. This seeming departure from the NUWSS's

traditional non-party stance was viewed by Mrs Fawcett, in Leslie Hume's words, as 'no more than passing political convenience that linked suffragists to the Labour Party; the alliance was in no sense intended as permanent, nor did it imply any loss of the NUWSS independence of action'. [23] The EFF, and its regional committees, began to propagandise for women's suffrage among the trade unions and, by setting up a non-paying Friends of Women's Suffrage, to establish a foothold in the working class.

Relationships between the Labour Party and NUWSS were not without their challenges, but the EFF undoubtedly brought things closer to the goal of the inclusion of women's suffrage in the Franchise and Registration Bill, now the only remaining opportunity for the enactment of women's suffrage. However, by January 1913 the Bill had been withdrawn and the NUWSS had finally abandoned all hope of obtaining women's suffrage by anything less than a government Bill; thus their main interest from then till the outbreak of war was on the next General Election, working with all political parties. However, an equally important aim during 1913-14 was to keep women's suffrage before the British public and make it a popular cause through the EFF, the Friends of Women's Suffrage, the appointment of working-class organisers, and working with trade unions. The last and most impressive piece of propaganda undertaken by the NUWSS – indeed arguably 'the most impressive demonstration for women's suffrage ever staged in Britain' [24] – was the 'Pilgrimage for women's suffrage'

15. Millicent Fawcett speaking at the Hyde Park rally, 26 July 1913

in July 1913. This was a march of converging groups of NUWSS members from every part of Britain, with meetings all along the route and culminating in a gathering of 70,000 in Hyde Park and a service in St Paul's. A considerable amount of money was raised. In 2013, a drama company called Dreadnought South West produced a play entitled *Oxygen*, which recreated the 1913 Pilgrimage with performances all over southwest England.

Most of Millicent Fawcett's campaigning at this period was done as president of the NUWSS, but the London Society for Women's Suffrage (Fawcett's predecessor body) played a very active part in NUWSS activities. Ray Strachey was herself a key player in the development of the Society and gives a vivid, near contemporary description of its work at this time. After their reorganisation in 1907 and move to larger premises at 58 Victoria Street:

> The years which followed were the great years of the Suffrage Movement. Enthusiasm was at white heat, and new recruits, new workers and new speakers poured in to all the societies almost faster than they could be absorbed. The income and membership of the London Society went up from £789 and 714 members in 1905, to £4,167 and 4000 members in 1912. Great efforts were made to arouse public opinion not only in the big National demonstrations, but in thousands of small stalls and meeting places, at street corners and in parks and open spaces. Leaflets, arguments and articles flooded, and sometimes choked up, the reading capacities of the public … For the London Society in particular the years 1908-1914 meant tremendously hard work. These years saw the first open-air Demonstration, the Mud March of 1907, and also the elaborate and beautiful processions which followed it. These Demonstrations owed their picturesque and dignified quality to the skilled work of the Artists' League for Women's Suffrage, which had been organised by Miss Mary Lowndes, a member of the Committee of the London Society. Under the direction of this

16. A view of the NUWSS Albert Hall meeting on 13 June 1908, Daily Graphic, *15 June 1908*

League banners and emblems of real beauty were made for the Societies all over the country, and when these were skilfully marshalled together in London the effect was something quite new in political demonstrations.

…[T]hese occasions revealed the growing enthusiasm for the cause which was springing up in London and all over the country. There was a remarkable series of Albert Hall meetings, which coincided with the organisation and enrolment of 20,000 non paying members who were called Friends of Women's Suffrage and with the establishment of 62 London Branches. There was the great Voters' Petition of 1910, when the London Society manned the approaches to the Polling Stations in 51 Constituencies, obtaining signatures through the snow and hail of a December election, and there were arduous bye-lection campaigns, notably those in Wimbledon and East St. Pancras where Mr. Bertrand Russell and Mr. Herbert Jacobs stood as Women Suffrage candidates. At this same time the Men's League for Women's Suffrage was formed with the object of helping all the Women's Suffrage Societies.[25]

LONDON SOCIETY FOR WOMEN'S SUFFRAGE.
DEMONSTRATION, JUNE 13th.

1. Will you walk in the Procession?
2. Will you drive in the Procession?
3. Will you take or sell tickets for the Albert Hall Meeting, Price, 5/-, 2/6, 1/- 6d?
4. Will you contribute towards the Demonstration Fund?
5. Can you bring any friends to walk in the Procession?
6. Could you offer hospitality to supporters coming from other parts of England?

Signature

Address

17. A disgruntled response: graffiti drawn on an invitation card to the NUWSS demonstration and procession, 13 June 1908

The year 1908 saw the start of what was to become a tradition of 'vanning', taking the suffrage message out on the road to towns and villages all over England in specially adapted caravans, drawn in one case by a horse called 'Asquith'. If the WFL established this tradition, the NUWSS took it up most enthusiastically and with great success, cheered by warm welcomes and enthusiastic meetings along the way.

Other actions taken by the Society included contacting some three hundred influential male supporters and asking them to interview or write to MPs, sending 'circulars to all its members requesting them to write letters on behalf of the [Conciliation] bill to members of the Government'. It also sponsored meetings, organised deputations to MPs, and in June 1910 'hired fifty sandwichmen to picket Whitehall with placards in support of the bill.'[26] Kate Parry Frye's *Suffrage Diary* (although she worked for the New Constitutional Society For Women's Suffrage, rather than the LSWS) gives a graphic description of the grinding hard work involved in organising for the suffrage at local, grassroots level – making contacts, booking rooms and speakers for meetings, writing letters, keeping accounts, distributing leaflets, endlessly tramping the streets in all weathers.[27]

And then on 4 August 1914 came the start of the First World War and everything changed.

SUFFRAGE COLOURS[1]

The original, best-known suffrage colours are of course the purple, white and green of the Women's Social and Political Union, chosen, probably by Emmeline Pethick-Lawrence, in May 1908 in preparation for the WSPU Hyde Park demonstrations on 21 June. White was for purity, green for hope, youth or regeneration, and purple for dignity, loyalty or courage. If purple can be reconceptualised as violet, this translated into the slogan Give Women Votes and did much to provide a focus for the militant suffragette movement.

The National Union of Women's Suffrage Societies had been using the colours red and white in 1907 and 1908 but in 1909 were urged by the suffragist publication Common Cause to add the colour green (which yielded the slogan Give Women Rights) to help to forge a constitutional identity – and badges, ribbons, flags and banners in the new colours flooded the constitutional market 'as an attempt to forge a constitutional identity in the face of militant notoriety … It is more and more imperative in these days that the fact that Constitutional Suffragists are greatest in numbers and widely spread should be known everywhere'.[2]

Other parts of the suffrage movement adopted slightly different colours – green, white and gold for the Women's Freedom League, purple, white and red for the Pethick-Lawrences' Votes for Women Fellowship, blue and silver for the Artists Suffrage League, pink and green for the Actresses' Franchise League, and purple, white, green and gold for Sylvia Pankhurst's East London Federation,

Each of these organisations considered their chosen colours hugely significant and important but most disappeared when the organisation died at some point during the twentieth century. Fawcett has remained true to the green, white and red colours although it is undoubtedly true that it is the purple, white and green that have seized the popular imagination. In 1998 there was a debate over whether Fawcett should abandon the green, white and red in favour of the ubiquitous green, white and purple. This evoked some strong emotions. A long-standing Fawcett member, Anne Walton, wrote passionately:

> While I take the point that the purple, green and white are undoubtedly identified by those who have a superficial knowledge of the women's movement with the suffrage campaign, we are not the 'Pankhurst Society'. There is, I believe an important principle at stake. We are perpetuating the ethos of the suffragists in that we still operate constitutionally and do not step outside the law as the suffragettes did. I think the message is an important one which I would like to see put forward with the greatest clarity.[3]

The debate was won in favour of green, white and red. We saw how green, white and red were worn at the official opening to Fawcett House and Fawcett seeks to sustain this tradition until today.

Chapter 3

Loyal citizens: the First World War, links with the peace movement and the Representation of the People Act 1918

We have seen how the years before the war were full of hectic campaigning for the vote by both the WSPU and the NUWSS. But it is ironic that having put itself on a 'war footing' in peacetime, the WSPU in wartime did just the opposite. On 15 August 1914, Mrs Pankhurst sent a circular to the Union's members:

> It is obvious that even the most vigorous militancy of the WSPU is for the time being rendered less effective by contrast with the infinitely greater violence done in the present war not to mere property and economic prosperity alone, but to human life…[1]

Under all the circumstances it had been decided to economise the Union's energies and financial resources by a temporary suspension of activities.

The suspension of militancy turned out to be more than temporary. Emmeline and Christabel poured their considerable energies into fighting the 'German peril', helping to recruit women into the munitions industry and assisting the war effort in every way possible, even, in 1915, re-christening *The Suffragette* newspaper as a vehicle for war propaganda, aptly titled *Britannia*. Many members objected to this diversion into 'new channels' from their main purpose, but were overruled by Emmeline. Finally, in 1917, the WSPU was wound up and its remaining funds put into an adoption home for female children. All this looks like an extraordinary volte face on the part of Christabel and her mother, but it can be argued that 'in fact the position the leaders took was entirely consistent with the political trajectory of an organisation that sought a Conservative government, sympathised with the Ulster Loyalists, and explicitly rejected the involvement of working-class women.'[2] Meanwhile, Sylvia Pankhurst had a very different war. Her East London Federation of the suffragettes not only continued to fight for the suffrage but also appealed to class anger against the war, organised community resistance partly through Sylvia's newspaper *The Women's Dreadnought*, resisted sweated labour, supported conscientious objectors and set up a network of radical welfare initiatives (cost-price restaurants, nurseries, art classes, and so on) for those adversely affected by the war. Sylvia was very sympathetic to the International Congress of Women meeting at The Hague,[3] and indeed is listed as one of the 180 British women wanting to attend the Congress.[4] She was also elected to the executive of the Women's International League, the British section of WILPF in 1915.[5]

The response of Mrs Fawcett and the suffragists was, at least initially, more nuanced. In July 1914, as the politicians moved towards the declaration of war, Mrs Fawcett, as vice-president of the International Women's Suffrage Alliance (IWSA), delivered an International Manifesto of Women to the foreign embassies in London. This declared that:

> We, the women of the world, view with apprehension and dismay the present situation in Europe which threatens to involve one continent, if not the whole world, in the disasters and the horrors of war … We women of twenty-six countries, having banded together in the International Women's Suffrage Alliance with the object of obtaining political means of sharing with men the power which shapes the fate of nations, appeal to you to leave untried no method of conciliation or arbitration for arranging international differences which may help to avert deluging half the civilised world in blood.[6]

Shortly afterwards, on 4 August 1914, IWSA and NUWSS came together to organise a mass meeting in London to allow women and women's organisations to protest against the war. The European women who attended this conference from all over Europe called for a negotiated settlement of the conflicts and utterly condemned the senseless war-driven destruction of a woman's family and her beloved land.[7]

All over Europe work on the suffrage was dwindling to be replaced by charity and relief work, for instance, with destitute Belgian refugees. In New York there was a great women's peace parade on 29 August. The IWSA meeting due in Berlin in June 1915 had to be cancelled, with a suggestion that it should be held alternatively in Holland, a neutral country. The UK committee of NUWSS voted in favour of this taking place, with only two exceptions, one of them their president, Millicent Fawcett. By March 1915 the international committee of IWSA voted against calling this conference by eleven to six. Many people feel disappointed with Millicent Fawcett over her stand but she was a patriot, this was entirely in accord with her response to the Boer War in 1899, which she saw as a 'fight for freedom', and by this stage in 1914 she believed it was right to lend the support of her organisations to the war effort – even to a Liberal government which had been lamentable in support of votes for women, and however much pain the war might cause her. She also received a threatening letter from Lord Robert Cecil.[8]

When this planned conference – the International Congress of Women – became one organised by individual women (one of them Chrystal Macmillan, recording secretary of IWSA) for individual women, Millicent took no part in its organisation or exe-

cution. But in spite of lack of support from suffrage leaders and bitter criticism from the press (who called the peace women 'peacettes' with some contempt), 180 British women applied for passports to attend the gathering, In the event, twenty-four passports were granted but only three women – Chrystal Macmillan, Kathleen Courtney and Emmeline Pethwick-Lawrence – actually made it to The Hague This was as much to do with the blocking tactics of the British government as with the hazards of attack by German submarines.

The three-day programme started in The Hague on 28 April 1915 and discussed twelve resolutions. It was attended by 1,200 women from twelve countries, including belligerent and neutral countries. In the event twenty resolutions were passed under seven headings:

1. Women and war
2. Actions towards peace
3. Principles of permanent peace
4. International co-operation
5. The education of children
6. Women and the Peace Settlement Conference
7. Action to be taken

18. The platform of the International Congress of Women, The Hague, 1915

Congress provided an analysis of the causes of war. Resolutions dwelt on the horrors of war and its specific effects on women. Actions suggested focussed on international justice and the full participation of women in creating a permanent peace. The principles of such a peace incorporated respect for nationality, arbitration and conciliation, international pressure, democratic control of foreign policy, and the enfranchisement of women. This was extremely progressive policy-making, but women were afraid their voices would not in fact be heard in the negotiations over the peace talks; nor would

their post-war needs be met. So they proposed that a delegation of women from the Congress should carry the messages expressed in the resolutions to the rulers of the belligerent and neutral nations of Europe and to the president of the United States, urging all governments to put an end to the bloodshed and begin peace negotiations. In all, fifteen countries were visited by two delegations which included Jane Addams, the American president of the Congress, and Chrystal Macmillan. They were received by twenty-four ministers, two presidents, one king and the Pope – in all cases sympathetically – and held public meetings to try to reach a peaceful resolution to the conflict. However, in spite of their passionate calls for peace and a manifesto that proposed a neutral conference for mediation, no action was actually taken by any head of state and the war continued unabated. In 1919, once the war was over, there was another large gathering of women – brought together first in Paris, then relocated to Zurich (German and Austrian women not being allowed to enter France) – which 'shadowed' the main peace conference in Paris. They were scathing about the punitive terms of the Treaty of Versailles, which included crippling reparations.

The Women's International League for Peace and Freedom (WILPF) was 'born out of profound dismay at the unjust outcome of Versailles'[9] and the need to find a peace that would endure. WILPF has been campaigning for peace ever since and celebrated its centenary in 2015 (taking The Hague Conference as its starting point and returning to The Hague in celebration and remembrance in 2015).

While sections of the women's movement were struggling to secure a peace, most of society in Britain was gripped by a desire to help the war effort – and the NUWSS as much as any. This took many forms – meeting the welfare needs of soldiers, providing Voluntary Aid Detachment staff (VADS) to hospitals, organising Red Cross centres and supporting the formation of special medical units. War needs changed as the enlistment of large numbers of men brought a great shortage of workers. The women's societies undertook the task of supplying 'women recruits for all kinds of work hitherto done only by men; and in this branch of the work the London Society, with which Mrs Fawcett was always in very close touch, became especially expert'. Their Women's Service Bureau opened in the first week of the war and 'was the means of drafting thousands upon thousands of women into new work, of the most varied kind'.[10]

Ray Strachey, the historian of the London Society and a near contemporary of Millicent Fawcett, whom she considered a mentor, describes the way in which the work of the Bureau intensified. It was accommodated in the voluntary workers' room of the old office in 58 Victoria Street and 'within a few weeks an enormous volume of work was centred upon it. Belgian refugees, War Relief Committees, Red Cross units, Hospital Stores, Canteens … were organised and staffed from that centre.' As the war progressed, '(t)he stress and intensity of all these activities was so great that the office was constantly busy till late at night, and the number of workers grew so enormously that two other large sets of rooms had to be secured in Victoria Street.[11]

An appeal leaflet, to raise £10, 000, on 'Women's Service' from April 1916 spells out the aim and scope of the Service:

- To enrol the many educated women willing and able to render national service during the present crisis, and, after careful selection, to place them in posts where their particular qualifications will be of most value to the country.
- To train women, by means of short courses, to supply the need of semi-skilled workers in aircraft and munition factories.
- To give women an opportunity for full and thorough training in professions and trades in which there is the prospect of a shortage, permanent or temporary.
- To send women to take part in the great work of relieving the suffering of the sick and wounded overseas.

Work, and the training for work, on offer varied from nursing to dentistry to munitions (and our television screens were full of images of women in munitions factories in the centenary year of 2014), to welding (oxy-acetylene welding was considered particularly appropriate for women), to plumbing and electrical fitting, to working on the land and later on to the WAAC, the WRNS and the WRAF (in whose original formation the Society was repeatedly consulted). This 'war work' was most prominent in London,

20. Women's Service Bureau welding school, 1914-18

organised by the London Society for Women's Suffrage, but also took place through other members of NUWSS all round the country. In Edinburgh, for instance, Dr Elsie Inglis set up a fully equipped hospital staffed by women – the famous Scottish Women's Hospital Unit. Initially all funds for this unit were raised by the Scottish Union of Women's Suffrage Societies, but it was later supported by the NUWSS. When she offered her services to the War Office, Elsie had been told: 'My good lady, go home and sit still', but by the end of the war the unit had served with distinction in France, Serbia, Russia, Salonica and Macedonia. The Scottish Hospitals not only provided urgently needed expert medical care on the front line but also demonstrated how women could cope with the dangers and rigours of war.

But while women were acquiring new skills which allowed them to contribute to the national emergency, the London Society realised they also 'deserved equal pay, equal treatment and fair conditions'[12] – issues that have stayed at the top of Fawcett's agenda ever since – so a political dimension developed to this work. Having abandoned the fight for the suffrage at the beginning of the war, Millicent Fawcett and the suffragists found it was now given back to them, as it were, as the suffrage movement once more became active in Parliament. Others had been keeping watch, and the Consultative Committee of Constitutional Women's Suffrage Societies had been meeting monthly from May 1916 to March 1919, monitoring government legislation and lobbying for women's rights when the opportunity arose.

The Speaker's Conference reported early in 1917 and the Representation of the People Bill was actively discussed and canvassed all through the following Spring, so that political work of the old kind had to be carried on in addition to the ever-growing war work. A fourth set of rooms was secured, organisers were re-engaged, and deputations, memorials and interviews were set on foot.

A new atmosphere of co-operation prevailed. Though success might be near,

the Society, remembering the disappointments of 50 years before, was determined to leave nothing to chance: Members of Parliament were rounded up as never before and Trade Unions, Municipal Authorities and the Press were all brought into play.[13]

21. Two WRNS fitting a mine, 1914-18

In March 1917, Millicent Fawcett led a deputation of representatives of twenty-four women's suffrage societies and ten other organisations to the new prime minister, Lloyd George, and on 10 January 1918 was present to witness the debate in the House of Lords that resulted in a majority for the women's suffrage clause to the Representation of the People Bill. Peers voting for the clause numbered 134, seventy-one peers voted against and thirteen abstained. The Representation of the People Bill was through both Houses and on 6 February received the royal assent and became the law of the land. It was certainly not everything women had been asking for: the vote was given only to women householders, unmarried or widowed ladies with property and the wives, over the age of thirty, of male local government electors. But compared with the total failure of the last fifty years it was a massive cause for celebration.

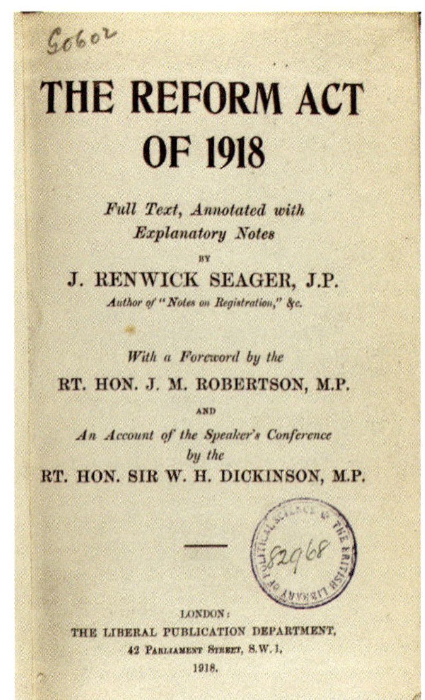

There was symbolism in the fact that the House of Commons chose to remove the grille in the Ladies Gallery which had only added to women's exclusion. Metaphorically and physically women were now on the way to being full participants in the political process.

22. The Representation of the People Act, 1918

Chapter 4

From suffrage to service: the Equal Franchise Act 1928 and the death of Millicent Fawcett

The First World War may have been a time of incomparable suffering and loss but at least it did at last bring votes for women – or some women. This gain was soon followed in November 1918 by legislation, initiated by the government, making women eligible (at the age of twenty-one) to be nominated and elected to the House of Commons. This bill went through very rapidly, much to the suffragists' surprise and delight, but it left little time for women to put themselves forward for election at the general election that took place in December 1918. In the event most of those who did stand did so as independents. One exception, and the only one to be elected, Countess Markievicz of the Irish Republicans, never took her seat, refusing to take the oath to the British king, so the first post-war parliament still had no women in it. Christabel Pankhurst stood for the coalition but was not elected and did not stand again. Instead she became a preacher, particularly in America, announcing the Second Coming.

The suffragists were concerned about how far their organisations should remain entirely concerned with the 'feminist' advancement of women (including achieving the full vote) and how far they should broaden out to include subjects like the welfare of children, improvements in health, education and sanitation, the enhancement of international understanding and education for women in citizenship. This was a long and impassioned argument and ended in a compromise. The National Union of Women's Suffrage Societies – NUWSS – became the National Union of Societies for Equal Citizenship – NUSEC. This remained feminist as before but with the added purpose 'to educate women in the duties of citizenship' – i.e. to ensure that once they had the vote they used it responsibly. Mrs Fawcett resigned as president of the NUWSS in 1919 and was replaced by Eleanor Rathbone. Meanwhile the London Society for Women's Suffrage decided to concentrate both on achieving the full vote and on the economic side of women's lives, changing its name at the 1919 AGM to the London Society for Women's Service (LSWS).

The challenge to women's economic lives was only too apparent in the years following the end of the war as men returned from the front and displaced the women who had so ably filled their jobs for the duration. In Ray Strachey's words: 'The London Society had upon its hands the demobilised war workers and faced the prospect of the terrible slump in women's labour which was bound to follow the return of the fighting men'.[1] (One could accurately say 'demoralised' as well as 'demobilised', since the end of the war brought women's financial prosperity to a complete halt.) Its Women's Service Bureau managed to stay open for another two years, but the days of mass mobilisation of women into work were well and truly over.

Nevertheless, even in this bleak scenario, there were signs of hope. Women might be losing jobs in thousands but there was evidence that the position of women had changed. As Strachey said in *Women's Suffrage and Women's Service*: 'Gone were the days when it was "not nice" to do paid work'.[2] Elsewhere she analysed the situation, pointing out that

… the occupations in which there were no strong men's unions did not lose women altogether. Here and there, … a few specially useful women were retained in almost all the new posts, and the tradition of their eligibility remained unbroken. Banks and commercial houses, Government offices and private firms, and a great host of miscellaneous occupations remained theoretically open.[3]

But for most women it was a time of extreme discouragement and disappointment. For the decade after the end of the First World War the women's organisations came together to attempt to ameliorate this situation. The LSWS in particular devoted itself to the cause of women's equality before the law, particularly in the field of employment and equal pay.

The result of all this effort was what Strachey called 'a big harvest of results'[4] in legislative and other terms. The Emancipation Bill of April 1919, initiated by the Labour Party and intended to remove at one sweep all the remaining disabilities of women, was eventually thrown out by the House of Lords. But the government then introduced their own Sex Disqualification Removal Bill, which opened the legal profession in all its branches to women, led to the immediate appointment of women magistrates and made women liable for jury service. It also secured the opening to women as of right of such bodies as the Society of Chartered Accountants. In 1919, Nancy Astor became the first woman to sit in the House of Commons after a by-election in Plymouth made necessary by her husband's accession to the peerage. She was treated with delighted enthusiasm by the hundreds of women who wrote to her for help. Meanwhile, after the extension of the local government franchise to married women, there was a remarkable increase in the number of local women councillors. In 1919, following the Peace Conference in Paris, the equal treatment of women was secured in the Covenant of the League of Nations and the eligibility of all women to all posts in the League and secretariat was assured. Back at home a prolonged battle took place for women's access to the Civil Service – where obstruction began to take the place of open opposition – and for equal pay for teachers. The latter was not successful.

In the House of Commons Nancy Astor was joined in 1921 by a Liberal woman, Mrs Margaret Wintringham, with whom, in spite of their belonging to different parties, she worked closely on 'women's causes'. By 1923 there were eight women members of Parliament, and women began to be represented on many important bodies, including the League of Nations Assembly.

The progressive legislation continued. In 1922, the Law of Property Act made husbands and wives, mothers and fathers, sons and daughters equal in cases of intestacy (thus redressing a great and old injustice). The Maintenance Act of 1922 was an important step for women, followed in 1923 by an act which increased the maximum contributions of fathers for their illegitimate children. The employment of women police, started in the war, continued with excellent results and this contributed to the setting up of the Criminal Law Commission in 1922 with Nancy Astor as a member The time was now right for her to build on Josephine Butler's earlier work on the Contagious Diseases Act with little controversy. Before she died in 1921, the educational pioneer Emily Davies was to see the culmination of her life's work with the award of degrees to women at Oxford in 1920 (although not at Cambridge). (See Box on education.)

Further legislation followed. In 1923, the Matrimonial Causes Act altered the grounds upon which divorce could be obtained, by making them the same for men and women. In 1925 and 1926 there were several more acts of great importance to women: the Guardianship of Infants Act (giving women the same rights as men over their offspring), the Widows' Pensions Act (which took widows out of the Poor Law and gave them a pension in their own right), and the Summary Jurisdiction Act (which removed difficulties in the administration of separation and maintenance orders). The Adoption of Children Act (lessening the undeserved misfortune of the child born out of wedlock) and the Midwives and Maternity Homes Act (which aimed to improve the conditions in which babies were born) covered the position of children. The Criminal Justice Act of 1926 almost completed the legal separation of married people into two individuals, an aim long advocated by the women's movement.

This was all progressive and much-required change, but underpinning it all was the need to lower the voting age from that of thirty as enshrined in the Representation of the People Act of 1918 (a restriction that was partly intended to keep the number of women voters below that of men). In 1924 a Conservative government came to power and declared its intention of remedying this anomaly. Mrs Fawcett weighed in with a letter to the *Times* of 6 June 1924 on the subject of the age limit for women voters.

Sir, – A few days ago I attended the sitting of Standing Committee A of the House of Commons, which is now considering the amending Bill now before the House which has for its main object the reduction of the absurdly high age limit for women voters. I was amazed to hear several Conservative members of

the Committee urge that there had been something equivalent to an honourable understanding in which the principal suffrage societies had concurred at the time when the whole subject of the Representation of the People Bill (1918) was before the Speaker's Conference, that the age limit of 30 would be left undisturbed for 'at least ten years'.

This view is in direct opposition to the actual facts …

… [T]hough the Speaker's Conference Report represented the near approach of the victory of Women's Suffrage, it was not treated by any of the Suffrage Societies as sacrosanct; no word was ever heard then of there being 'an honourable obligation' to remain petrified for ten years.[5]

The suffragist and feminist organisations began to press Stanley Baldwin, the new prime minister, to fulfil his promise to abolish the age bar for women. The Bill went ahead with very little opposition, although some (certainly not Mrs Fawcett) felt that young women (who were about to be enfranchised) were not to be trusted. Fortunately this opposition was not enough to delay the legislation. In the King's speech of February 1928 the Bill to equalise the franchise was prominent. It was presented as a government measure on 29 March 1928, and received the support of both the opposition parties. The second reading was carried by 387 votes to ten. On 23 May the Bill passed the House of Lords by a large majority. 'With the passage of this Act the last glaring inequality in the legal position of women was abolished'.[6] Baldwin wrote to Millicent Fawcett on 5 August 1928 to express his satisfaction with the outcome.[7]

Most readers of this book would probably argue about the term 'last glaring inequality' as they grapple with myriad equality issues of the twenty-first century, but there is no doubt it was a massive achievement, which brought to an end sixty-two years of

25. Celebrating the Equal Franchise Act, 1928: Millicent Fawcett, Philippa Fawcett, Agnes Garrett and Ray Strachey

campaigning, years dominated by one woman, Millicent Garrett Fawcett. She had been in the House of Commons to hear John Stuart Mill introduce his suffrage amendment in 1867 and was now in the House of Lords to hear the full suffrage 'on the same terms as men' finally approved. This did not mean all the Lords approved it and many accepted 'in a spirit of resignation', but accept it they had to and did. This gave Millicent Fawcett enormous pleasure. She went home 'with a thankful heart' and that night wrote 'I have had extraordinary good luck in having seen the struggle from the beginning'.[8] The Royal Assent was finally given on 2 July.

Millicent had already been made a Dame in 1925 (as well as having been awarded earlier honorary degrees) and now had more than a year to enjoy the further pleasures of victory. Summer 1928 was full of thanksgiving services, parties, meetings at all of which her presence was urgently required and from which she came away laden down with flowers. Her last year was also spent travelling, writing and promoting various feminist causes, including the Elizabeth Garrett Anderson Hospital established by her sister, campaigning for the Age of Marriage Act, passed in May 1929, and for the education of girls in India. She had given up the presidency of NUWSS when it became NUSEC but she remained closely involved with the LSWS as it moved into its new premises in Marsham Street (see Chapter 5). The laying of the foundation stone for their new buildings in Westminster on 24 April 1929 turned out to be one of her last public acts before she died on 5 August.

Millicent Fawcett's death was greeted with great grief not just in women's organisations but by the establishment and the population at large. There was a deep understanding of the contribution that her quiet persistence had made not only to women but to society as a whole. The *Manchester Guardian* of 7 August 1929 set the tone:

> There were three stages in the emancipation of women. The first was the long campaign of propaganda and organisation, at the centre of which, patient, unwearying, and always hopeful, stood Dame Millicent. The second was the campaign of the Militants, which, since it depended on sensation, brought to the movement the enthusiastic attention of the popular press. The third was the war. Had there been no militancy and no war the emancipation of women would still have come, although more slowly. But without the faithful preparation of the ground over many years by Dame Millicent Fawcett and her colleagues, neither militancy nor the war would have produced the crop.

The London Society felt her loss particularly keenly and their minute books are full of arrangements to remember her. On 2 October, the Committee 'stood in silence to honour the memory of their late President', but they were already discussing her memorial service in Westminster Abbey, designed so that the whole nation could honour her. A Memorial Service Committee was set up to organise and collect money for this event, which took place on 19 November 1929. On 4 December, Lady Cynthia Colville conveyed to the Committee the Queen's appreciation of Dame Millicent's remarkable qualities. By March 1930, LSWS and NUSEC had set up a Joint Committee to plan the erection of a memorial plaque in Westminster Abbey, alongside that by Alfred Gilbert to her husband Henry Fawcett after his death in 1884.

The LSWS minutes of the next two years are dominated by plans for this plaque, conducted both with the powers-that-be at Westminster Abbey and with the chosen sculptor Sir Herbert Baker. In the midst of all this there was a suggestion from NUSEC that Millicent Fawcett might be better remembered by a foundation benefiting women rather than a memorial. This was overruled but it was agreed that any money left over should go to women's causes.

The discussion over the form the memorial should take continued with particular debate with the Abbey over the inscription. In the end the words

A wise, constant and courageous Englishwoman
She won citizenship for women

were agreed . On 12 March 1932, the day of the unveiling of the memorial in the chapel of the Holy Cross (re-named St George's chapel that same year), the *Times* Art Critic described it in these terms:

> The Dame Millicent Garrett Fawcett memorial to be unveiled today in Westminster Abbey is a very good example of discreet addition. Designed by Sir Herbert Baker, A.R.A., in collaboration with Mr. A.G. Walker, A.R.A., and Mr. Laurence Turner, it takes the form of two circular bronze plaques with wreaths and inscriptions in relief, each plaque having a pendant enamelled decoration – the Order of the British Empire and the badge of the National Union of Women's Suffrage Societies respectively. These plaques are attached to the springing of the arch which encloses the memorial to Henry Fawcett. If memory can be trusted, this is the only instance in the Abbey of a combined memorial to husband and wife.[9]

The actual unveiling was carried out by Viscount Cecil of Chelwood, a long-time supporter of women's suffrage and president of the LSWS. He gave a glowing eulogy to Dame Millicent:

> [Mrs Fawcett] passed almost the whole of her life in pursuit of one great purpose, the emancipation of women. She strove for their higher education, for an equal opportunity with men, and ultimately there was the climax for their enfranchisement to be full citizens of the country. She lived to see almost the whole of the objects for which she strove actually accomplished. That was a very great, and, as human affairs went, a rare success.

26. Memorial plaque to Millicent Fawcett in its former position in St George's chapel, Westminster Abbey, 2008.

… [S]he was a leader, and was followed, because every one trusted her. She was absolutely single-minded. She never faltered, and she never looked back …[10]

Millicent Fawcett did not achieve the accolade of a life-size statue as Emmeline Pankhurst had in 1930 in Victoria Tower Gardens alongside the House of Lords, but her more modest memorial in Westminster Abbey became the focus of an annual commemorative service organised by the Fawcett Society to remember Millicent with gratitude, affection and pride. This has been one of the most important points on Fawcett's calendar, although from 2010 to 2014 the ceremony had to be held elsewhere, at the Suffragette Fellowship Monument in Christchurch Gardens in Victoria Street in Westminster, while St George's chapel was renovated.[11] Fawcett , however, was back in the chapel for the 2015 commemoration.

Chapter 5

Rooms of their own: the Fawcett Society and the Millicent Fawcett Hall

This chapter will focus on the first purpose-built buildings for the women's movement in Britain: the Millicent Fawcett Hall in Westminster in London, and the other buildings in Westminster situated between Marsham and Tufton streets used by the predecessor body to the Fawcett Society. Under its previous name of the London and National Society for Women's Service, the Fawcett Society occupied the Hall for only ten years (from 1929 to 1939), although it was on the site – in other buildings down Marsham Street and Tufton Street – for more than thirty. It then spent nearly ten years half a century later, in the 1990s, trying to save the Hall from demolition and ensure the women's movement continued to have access to it. But even combined this is a short period – however important – in a history of 150 years, so I will also look more briefly at what led the Society to move to Marsham Street in 1924, where it had lived before that, and where it has lived since it finally left its offices in Tufton Street in 1956. A theme through all this will be the question that if, as Virginia Woolf argued, a room of her own was so essential for the woman who wanted to be a writer, how equally important were premises – rooms of their own – to women's organisations which wanted, in effect, to re-write the world for women.

Millicent Garrett Fawcett dominates this debate because although the Society did not finally name itself after her till 1953 (very wisely, since most previous names had been long-winded and often instantly forgettable – even the Hall started its life as the Women's Service Hall) – her life had a huge direct influence on the acquisition and design of these buildings. It was certainly the first time the Society had premises which could be called 'fit for purpose'. The list of their addresses from 1872 is a roll call of the temporary and the tatty which will be only too familiar to most women's organisations today.

Going back, there is evidence of suffragist activity in various places (e.g. in Elizabeth Garrett's sitting room or Mrs Mentia Taylor's house in the 1860s), but the first mention

WOMEN'S SERVICE HOUSE
35/37 MARSHAM STREET, WESTMINSTER, S.W 1

27. Women's Service House, view from the top window

of an 'address' of its own for the women's suffrage movement seems to come in 1872, when the minute book of the Central Committee of the National Society for Women's Suffrage reveals that they were based at 9 Berners Street, north of Oxford Street, moving in 1875 to 64 Berners Street at a rent of £70 per annum. They were still in 64 Berners Street in 1881, worrying about a 'copy machine to be bought, not to exceed £3. Dangerous oilcloth on stairs to be replaced',[1] but by 1883 they had shifted to 29 Parliament Street in Westminster, where they stayed till the move to 10 Great College Street in 1889. For more than a century they were to remain within easy reach of Parliament (although they did go south of the Thames in 1982 to Harleyford Road in Vauxhall), until they moved to the Barbican area in 1995. They then went south of the river again in 2013 to Addington Square in Camberwell, back north (and east) to Bethnal Green in 2014 and then, in 2015, south once more to Union Street in Southwark.

During this period of hovering around Parliament, they were to occupy an array of different addresses, particularly up and down Victoria Street. In 1895 they were in 47 Victoria Street and in 1907 at number 25. Soon after, the reorganised London society moved into larger premises across the road to number 58 and remained there up to, through and after the First World War. Ray Strachey, the historian of the Society, has described the hectic days of expansion at the beginning of the war with the Women's Service Bureau and its multifarious contributions to the war effort (see Chapter 3). But these heady days were coming to an end. A lack of funds closed the Bureau early in 1922, the second office at 56 Victoria Street was given up, and in 1923, number 58 itself had to be ceded and a small temporary home found in Buckingham Gate.[2]

This peripatetic office life makes the move to Women's Service House in Marsham Street in 1924 even more significant. Its acquisition was made possible by a gift for £1,000 just when the Society was at its lowest financial ebb, and by the trust fund established by the same donor, Sarah Clegg, on the Society's sixtieth birthday on 18 November 1926. Here at last was a home of their own – big enough, fit for purpose

MILLICENT FAWCETT HALL.

(and it was to fulfil a wide range of purposes), within a stone's throw of Parliament – and, with the trust fund, permanent enough to be able to plan ahead. As Ray Strachey wrote: 'from the opening of this centre a new prosperity … new life; more money, more enthusiasm, more members and more hope began to flow into the Society.'[3]

The first move in 1924 was to the old disused Georgian pub The Fleece, with its famous ceramic sign, at 35 Marsham Street. The Annual Report for 1924, with Mrs Fawcett as president, was produced from there, and Women's Service House (WSH) was officially opened on 13 May. The opening was attended by Marion Crofton, an enthusiastic member of the London Society, whose scrapbooks track all the major events of these years.[4] It was in WSH that the Women's Service Library had its early beginnings in 1926 (see Chapter 7). It was also here that the Junior Council was set up, which was to be so influential over the next fifteen years and indeed to virtually steer the Society, since most new members came via the Council (see Chapter 6). The images the Women's Service House produced of itself are curiously charming. This might be arguably the first women's centre in the United Kingdom, but it is a very genteel one. However, there is nothing particularly genteel about their participation in the equal political rights demonstration in Hyde Park in July 1926 and their campaign for the Bill to equalise the franchise. Dame Millicent Fawcett (as she had been since 1925) was in retirement but she came to the House of Commons in July 1928 to see the Bill passed.

She was there also on 24 April 1929 to lay the foundation stone for the new buildings situated between Marsham and Tufton streets, which an increased gift from Sarah Clegg had given the Society the confidence to embark upon. This was a very ambitious and indeed lavish building project undertaken by the architect James Douglas Wood (there was some debate about why they did not use a woman architect, but one of the Junior Council's rising stars, Elizabeth Scott, did have some input and she was busy building the new Shakespeare theatre in Stratford-upon-Avon). The new hall with its distinguished distyle Ionic portico led into a four-bay hall; the bays were marked with pilasters rising from a wooden dado to a barrel-vaulted roof, and there was a stage with a wooden proscenium arch of curved acanthus leaf design. There was an extensive restaurant in the basement, with columns adorned with ram's mask capitals, a top-lit library, and a reading room. A separate entrance with an inscription gave access from

28. Millicent Fawcett Hall, so renamed in 1932

To meet Viscountess Astor, M.P., Viscount & Viscountess
Cecil of Chelwood & other friends & patrons of the Society.

THE LONDON & NATIONAL SOCIETY FOR WOMEN'S SERVICE
27, Marsham Street, Westminster.

The Chairman & Executive Committee

At Home

on Tuesday, 10th December, 1929, at 9.30 p.m.

at the formal opening of

Women's Service Hall,

46, Tufton Street, S.W.1.

by

ANNIE VISCOUNTESS COWDRAY.

R.S.V.P. to
The Secretary,
27, Marsham St., S.W.1.   Refreshments 1/-

entrance :
46, Tufton Street,
S.W.1.

29. Invitation to the opening of the Women's Service Hall, 10 Decmber 1929

Tufton Street, whose existing houses also formed part of the total scheme. Marion Crofton was there to see the laying of the foundation stone in a ceremony that certainly lived up to the buildings.

Arrangements for the ceremony were discussed at a special meeting of the Executive Committee on 16 April 1929. About two hundred people were to be accommodated. The minutes record the following:

> Mr Wood undertook to have a platform made where the stone would be laid for the principal guests, and to erect staging over the partially built room behind the shop, for about 50 people and to arrange the stage for as many more: also to put a small number of seats into the hall itself. A platform for the Press would be built over the stairs to the basement.

The meeting agreed to lay 'some documents and suffrage medals under the Foundation Stone'. Mr Wood undertook 'to procure a small box to contain these'. It was further agreed 'to provide a small string band' to play in the library as entertainment for early arrivals. The order of ceremony and of speeches was drawn up. Doubtless so as to make the most of fund-raising opportunities, members of the Appeal Committee were to be invited 'to join the Executive Committee in welcoming the Society's guests'. Finally the special meeting agreed 'to arrange a luncheon for 40 guests in the Library'.[5]

Sadly, Millicent Fawcett died in the summer of 1929, and Marion Crofton's next formal event for the Society seems to have been the service in her memory in Westminster Abbey on 19 November. Dame Millicent was thus not there on 10 December, when Marion was back for the formal opening of Women's Service House (with the address of its Tufton Street entrance). On 4 June 1931, Marion returned for another At Home, this time on the completion of the whole building, and on 12 March 1932, again in Westminster Abbey, for the unveiling of the memorial to Millicent Fawcett. On 22-23 November 1932, Marion was positioned at a stall in the Reading Room for two days for the Mart of London River, the Society's main fund-raising event, opened by Edith Evans one day and Rose Macaulay the other; the following year she was back, in 'her usual place', for the Mart, this time opened by Vera Brittain. She must have returned the next year because a note in her scrap book in November 1934 signed, affectionately and gratefully, by Philippa Strachey, secretary of the Society, 'assures her the help which you gave was quite invaluable'.

This was only the tip of the iceberg, since the Society made full use of its new facilities, and not just for its growing library and political campaigning on, for instance, the position of women in the Civil Service and municipal authorities, on the co-operation of women in the work of the League of Nations, the national health insurance bill and the nationality of married women. The growing Junior Council in particular used the premises as a kind of club. In addition to the restaurant there were rooms to stay in and the hall was constantly in use for performances, parties, plays (the Marsham Street Players became a regular feature), debates and talks on a wide range of topical subjects. (See Chapter 6.)

Speakers in the Millicent Fawcett Hall included Eleanor Rathbone, Ellen Wilkinson, Bertrand Russell, Margaret Bondfield (the first woman member of the cabinet), Vera Brittain and Virginia Woolf. The last was invited by her friend Philippa Strachey to share a platform with Dame Ethel Smyth to talk on 'Music and literature' on Wednesday, 21 January 1931. Woolf's speech, entitled 'Professions for women', was considered by her biographer Hermione Lee 'a public performance of great significance in the history of twentieth century feminism'.[6] Woolf described her route to becoming a writer, warned against the dreaded stereotype of the 'Angel in the house', which has done so much to hold women back, and recognised the 'obstacles and phantoms' which litter the path of women striving to enter professions. Her audience of two hundred included many distinguished guests (several of whom, including Vera Brittain, wrote the evening up in the press) and 'well dressed, keen and often beautiful young women'[7] – members of the Junior Council – whom she told: 'You have won rooms of your own in the house hitherto exclusively owned by men. You are able,

LONDON & NATIONAL SOCIETY FOR WOMEN'S SERVICE
29, Marsham Street, Westminster, S.W. 1.
Secretary: Miss Philippa Strachey.

MART OF LONDON RIVER

under the patronage of
THE VISCOUNTESS CECIL OF CHELWOOD

Millicent Fawcett Hall

46, Tufton Street, Westminster, S.W. 1.

NOVEMBER 22nd and NOVEMBER 23rd, 1933

Doors open 12 o'clock.

Formal Opening 2.30 p.m.

Wednesday, November 22nd, 1933, at 2.30 p.m. Opened by - MISS VERA BRITTAIN
Chairman: Mrs. Kinnell

Thursday, November 23rd, 1933, at 2.30 p.m. Opened by - - MISS JEAN CADELL
Chairman: Lady Sprigge

M.C. In the Usual Place

30. Invitation to the Mart of London River, 1933

though not without great labour and effort, to pay the rent … But this freedom is only a beginning … How are you going to furnish it … decorate it? With whom are you going to share it, and upon what terms?'[8]

This evening had a double effect – first the speech went on resonating for Virginia Woolf and found its way into books like *The Pargiters*, *The Years* and *Three Guineas*. But it also consolidated her relationship with the Society. Surprisingly for a 'non-joiner', she became a member in November 1932, in 1933 donated the manuscript of *A Room of One's Own* for Society funds, and in 1938 put her name to the Library Appeal. Thereafter her name regularly appears in the Library minutes as a donor of books.

The Millicent Fawcett Hall (as it became in July 1932, when the Junior Council complained that the name 'Women's Service' was not very enticing and 'Millicent Fawcett' would be much easier to market) and the whole centre was a source of great pride to the Society, but also, it must be said, of anxiety, particularly after Sarah Clegg died intestate in 1930. The buildings might be officially owned by the Trustees, and many people contributed with huge generosity to their furnishing and fitting-out, but there was never enough money to run them without worry. The Hall was considered 'potentially' a magnificent money-making possession. Parts of the building were let to tenants. Strong attempts were made to market it to outside bodies, and letters were sent

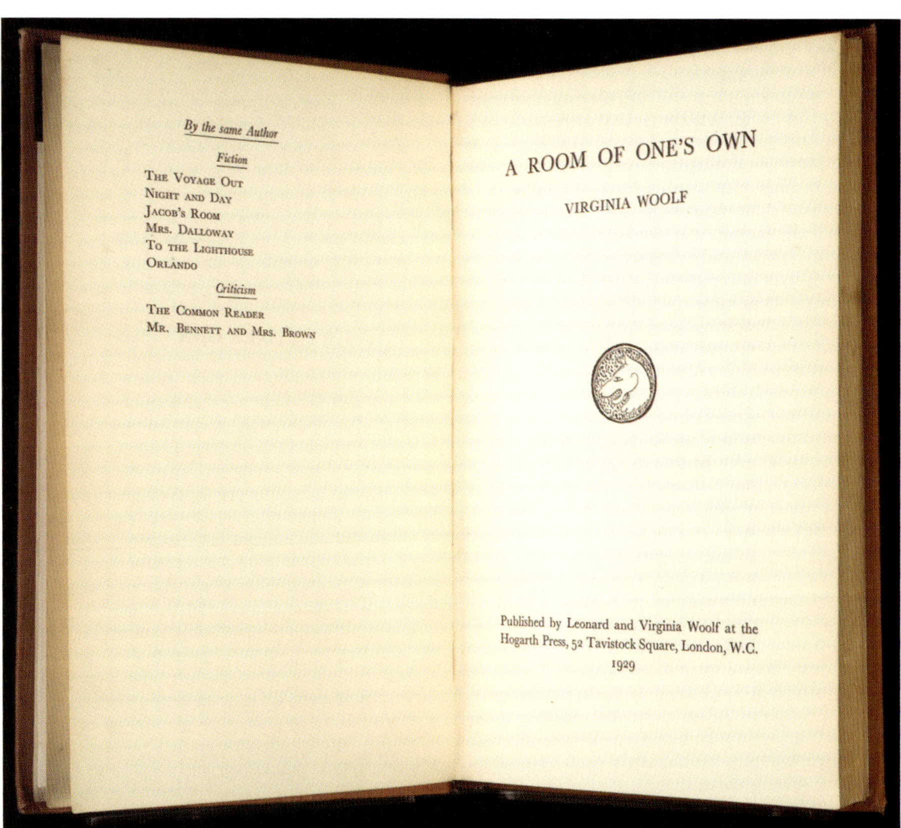

31. Virgina Woolf, A Room of One's Own, *1929*

WOMEN'S SERVICE HOUSE 35/37 MARSHAM STREET, WESTMINSTER, S.W.1

out extolling its virtues. Nonetheless, financial anxiety reverberates through the Society's minute books. Talk of deficits, emergencies and financial crises, calls for reduction of expenditure, increased fees, special appeals like the Guarantee Fund, staff asked to make special sacrifices, become repetitive. The annual November bazaar, the Mart of London River, plays a key part in the Hall's economy and often rescues a disastrous situation. Quite a lot of time that might have been spent on campaigning is spent worrying about simply funding the building.

Nevertheless, in spite of the financial problems it generated, the Hall in most ways had a marvellous decade. It was at the centre of feminist campaigning and public debate, the place to be, the focus and inspiration of its members, a home to the women's movement.

Years of struggle

All this comes to an end on 3 September 1939, when war breaks out. The decision is made to pack up the most valuable books and records, dispose of most of the staff and close the premises. A skeleton staff moves to Bedford College at Regent's Park in London, where the Society is offered space. The priorities of the Society are defined as to carry on the political campaign (which concentrates substantially on women and war work), sustain and expand the Junior Council and maintain the Library. After three months there is a partial return to Marsham Street, although under considerable difficulties and not to the Hall or restaurant, which have been 'de-rated', thus saving money. A sort of normality is re-established. The Library is re-opened. The Junior Council has a successful meeting in December, the Marsham Street Players agree to meet weekly (and later run fencing classes), lectures on art and society are given and,

32. The restaurant, Women's Service House

perhaps most significantly, the Friends of the Library is set up.

But in spite of heroic attempts to keep things going and some strong campaigning, basically the buildings and the Society have a dreadful war, with minute books[9] sounding like messages from the front line. On 11 October 1940, a landmine destroys all the front of Women's Service House although the Hall, Library and Members' Room suffer only from a broken door and windows and the contents of the Library are intact. Tenants demand termination of leases under the War Damages Act, and negotiations open with Westminster City Council about de-rating. Mr Wood, the architect of the Hall, is reported as having been of great assistance in making an immediate survey, arranging the removal of debris and shoring up the walls and preparing a claim for compensation for war damage. Number 35 Marsham Street has also suffered serious damage both internally and to the roof. Staff are temporarily laid off (again), and Miss Watts, the chairman [*sic*], offers temporary refuge in her offices in nearby Dartmouth Street. The main concern becomes to save the Library, which, having escaped so far, is still exposed to continual bombing. Miss Douie, who lives in Oxford, negotiates several offers from colleges there. In spite of split sites, to everyone's relief, it does well and attracts a devoted new following.

Back in London the Society is struggling. Their offices and committee rooms are in ruins and much of their contents destroyed or damaged and great confusion caused among the papers (in the circumstances it is amazing there are any archives at all left from this period). Some looting has also taken place. The office work is now being carried out in the Members' Room, the door and windows of which have been temporarily repaired. The financial situation is extremely serious as the bank has refused any further extension of the overdraft beyond the £100 needed to make the building weatherproof. The only other income, except for small and dwindling investments, comes from subscriptions, which have seriously dropped and must be expected to continue to do so, while there would remain certain expenses for rates and repairs, especially to 35 Marsham Street, for which they had responsibility till 1943. There are desperate attempts to sell off stock and meet liabilities.[10]

Some political work is being done in 'endeavouring to counteract the continued neglect to appoint women to responsible positions and continued differentiation in the relation of payments to the sex of the recipients', but there is regret that 'in present circumstances the Society could not do more'.[11]

Meanwhile, to add injury to everything else, Miss Blackwell, the assistant secretary, falls in the courtyard while on a visit and breaks an arm but gallantly 'continued to deal with the Society's correspondence'.[12] Philippa Strachey is based in Oxford but stays in Bedford College during the week. Another policy sub-committee reiterates the absolute priority of keeping the Library going till the end of the war and conserving funds to be able to re-open then. It is essential to reduce expenditure on salaries and the gallant Miss Blackwell is replaced by a cheaper clerk.

They carry on somehow in Marsham Street and on 9 June 1943, manage to hold their first General Meeting since 1938. There are very stirring resolutions:

- a call to the government to accept 'without reserve the participation of women in

the life of the nation on equal terms with men'
- a re-affirmation that the Society will 'promote equal opportunities and equal pay for men and women in work' and will press for
- the abolition of the marriage bar and 'the restoration to married women of the same rights in nationality as those of men and single women'
- a call to the government 'to act impartially in providing employment after demobilisation' and to 'give opportunity for the use of the varied capacities of women no less than those of men'
- a call to the Foreign Secretary 'to complete the modernisation of the foreign service … by opening it to women on the same terms as to men'

A further resolution was passed against trying to return women to the nursery and kitchen after the war.[13]

There is a small revival in membership and many offers of help and then Miss Strachey reports on the night of 14 March 1944, when 'incendiaries caused a serious fire in the upper part of Women's Service House facing Marsham Street. The roof and much of the top floor had been consumed and the staircase badly injured'. The rest of the building was drenched in water. '[O]ne incendiary bomb had come through the roof of the hall and burnt itself out on the floor.'[14] Mr Wood comes to the rescue again and once more they stay put, but in October 1944 they are back in Dartmouth Street 'in consequence of the damage to the office caused by flying bombs on 1 July 1944', when an 'exceedingly destructive bomb' – a V1 – had fallen in Tufton Street outside the entrance to the Millicent Fawcett Hall,[15] followed by a bomb on the opposite side of Marsham Street on 19 July. Mr Wood, after inspecting the premises, said that 'they could not be made fit for use again until after the war'. (But he does astonishingly manage to lease the restaurant as a 'dining centre for naval petty officers working for the French Admiralty', whose headquarters were nearby.)[16]

Miss Watts had most generously once more given hospitality to the Society in her office during this new emergency, but it is now clear that they have to abandon Marsham Street. They take out a lease on a room at 40 Broadway which is clean although with shabby linoleum (shades of the comment back in 1881 about dangerous oilcloth on the stairs!). This will be covered by rugs from Marsham Street, and curtains also brought from there[17] – while remaining furniture and files are stored in basements at Women's Service House. More than five years later these basements are reopened to find a looted 'scene of indescribable confusion' of broken furniture and glass, scattered and torn documents, photographs and paper with very little salvageable value.[18]

It continues to be a struggle, but in 1947, negotiations open for Westminster City Council to make a compulsory purchase of the whole site: 25, 27, 29 and 31 Marsham Street, including the Hall complex – number 35 was never owned by them – and the houses in Tufton Street, in order to set up what becomes the Abbey Community Centre, with Mr Wood being retained to give advice on the restoration of the property. The selling price starts at £65,000 but is pushed up to £80,000 with (as part of the deal) free accommodation for the Library in the Great Smith Street Public Library and a preferential seven-year lease on 50 Tufton Street. This was the unique brick-built

house dating from 1780–90 with its elliptical staircase and other features.

The loss of the Hall was obviously a sadness to the Society and the Trustees, but I think, after everything that had happened, it was probably also a relief. The Library could be brought back to London, the office moved to Tufton Street on 31 May 1950, the Millicent Fawcett Hall could be rented for meetings, and the money invested from the sale was estimated to bring in a crucial £1,300 a year, instead of a constant deficit. But the Society still wanted a home of its own and to be reunited with the Library and started looking at freehold properties as early as 1952. In 1957, the Fawcett Society, as it now was, bought a new home for itself at 27 Wilfred Street in Victoria – known as Fawcett House. This building inspired great affection. One enthusiastic member, Cynthia White, even wrote a poem about it which started:

33. Damage caused in Tufton Street from a V1 bomb in the vicinity of Millicent Fawcett Hall, July 1944

Once upon a winter's morning
Footsteps rang down Wilfred Street …

It went on:

Though the inner doors – and goodness!
What a hive of industry

Occupants at every table
All as busy as could be

And continued, affectionate stanza after affectionate stanza.[19]

By 1976, however, it was clear that the Society could no longer sustain either the house or the growing Library. Rehousing the latter appropriately became a matter of concern. In the end the choice came down to one between the London School of Economics and the City of London Polytechnic.[20] The Polytechnic was finally chosen, and the Fawcett Library moved in 1977 into its own space in the basement of the Polytechnic's building in Old Castle Street in Aldgate in east London. (See Chapter 7 for a fuller account of these negotiations and of the Library's subsequent history.)

This process of finding a home for the Library was accompanied by protracted and extremely complex negotiations on the legal status of the Women's Service Trust; these resulted finally in a legal victory in 1976, which declared the Trust valid and charitable, thus establishing for the first time the principle that equality between men and women can be a legitimate charitable aim.[21] Once this issue was resolved, the Society was able to sell Wilfred Street, for £95,000. It had a couple of short-term homes until it moved in 1982 to 46 Harleyford Road in Vauxhall, just south of the Thames. This location was hardly ideal, being a dark basement in the midst of a vast traffic system in an area many members found intimidating. One of them wrote to the Chair in 1985 that she was 'currently only willing to make the unpleasant trek because of great belief in Fawcett's aims'.[22]

The fight to save Millicent Fawcett Hall

It was at this point, in the late 1980s, that Marsham Street came back into Fawcett's life. By now the Abbey Community Centre, which had occupied the site since the Society left, had moved, and the premises had deteriorated further as a rough sleepers' shelter. Westminster City Council wanted to dispose of the site and placed it on the market. Fawcett and the National Alliance of Women's Organisations joined together under the leadership of Elizabeth Collingridge and the name of Project W, bringing as it were the weight of the wider women's movement, to put in a bid, prepared by Matrix Architectural Group and Women's Pioneer Housing, for multifunctional use of the site, including space for women's organisations. The bid got to the last two, at which point in October 1991 Westminster City Council withdrew it from the market because of the generally depressed state of the property market.

The fear now was that the council (led by Dame Shirley Porter) would knock down the buildings and turn them into a car park. They were in a very bad state. Squatters had moved in. Considerable damage had been caused and fittings, fireplaces and tiles removed, with an attempt to gouge out a decorative 1920s stair rail.

This situation rallied a huge number of different groups to save the site – not only the women's movement but groups such as the Thorney Island Society (under the indefatigable June Stubbs), Save Britain's Heritage, the Westminster Society, English Heritage, the London Society, and the Thirties Society, who did not want to see yet another piece of old Westminster disappear.[23] The battle to save the Millicent Fawcett

Hall took place on two fronts during the early part of 1992: firstly a very strong lobby of Westminster City Council with a massive letter-writing campaign, not just by all the groups mentioned above, but also by individuals including people like the Marquess of Anglesey who wrote: 'I hope this philistine, almost obscene proposal will be allowed to die the death which it richly deserves';[24] and secondly a more behind-the-scenes approach, supported by the architectural historian Dr Lynne Walker, to the newly formed Department of National Heritage to save the buildings by having them listed. It was also strongly written up in the press. Arguments were made on architectural, cultural and historical grounds: not only were the buildings worth preserving in their own right but they were the 'the sole remaining purpose-built building in London connected with the women's suffrage movement … they signify the village of Westminster and the birth of the suffrage movement around the corner from Parliament'.[25]

It was touch and go whether the listing would come through before the Council started pulling down the buildings. In the event, Millicent Fawcett Hall was the first building listed by the new Department of National Heritage, with Kathleen Halpin, ninety-five years old, who had been a key player in the Hall in the 1920s and 1930s, being much used in photographs and articles. The minister, Robert Key, rang Liz Collingridge personally to give her the news, but the more formal letter of 21 May 1992 to Dr Lynne Walker stated that the Millicent Fawcett Hall was 'of sufficient special architectural or historic interest to be listed – Grade II … the adjoining buildings were not, however, considered to merit listing'.[26] This decision meant sadly that both 35 Marsham Street and the houses in Tufton Street, including the beautiful elliptical staircase in number 50, were subsequently demolished for new flats and houses which now wrap round the Hall, with the only memory of their past in their name – Millicent Court.

While a huge effort was expended on saving the Hall, there was less unanimity about what to do with it once saved. Project W disbanded, and while some in the Fawcett Society felt that the Society should still try to buy the site, the majority, including their new director, Shelagh Diplock, felt this would be a potentially disastrous diversion from their main purpose – to be a cutting-edge campaigning organisation for women's equality. In the mid-1990s a new champion, Barbara Grundy of the Foundation for Women's Art, headed up a group of women's organisations initially brought together by Lesley Abdela under the banner of Women through the Millennium. She and Gail Waldman of Women in Architecture prepared an ambitious bid for funding to the Millennium Lottery to fund both an exhibition at the Dome and to develop the Marsham Street site as a women's centre. It was unfortunate that they were competing with the bid from the Women's Library, which was successful, while Women through the Millennium were not. But Barbara waited to see what would happen, feeling that all was not necessarily lost and there might be the potential to do some sort of a deal with the successful bidder. Westminster School soon emerged as the favoured bidder, and Barbara was able to work with them to build in access for Fawcett and the Foundation for Women's Art as a condition of the sale, up to a maximum of twelve times a year, in holidays or at half-term.

The Fawcett Society today is a very effective campaigning organisation, continuing to fight to close the inequality gap between men and women. After coming up from the basement in Harleyford Street in 1992 they shared modern office buildings around the Barbican. It is interesting that they chose to draw on the past in their office in Berry Street by naming their meeting room after Mary Stott, the journalist, feminist and enormous friend of Fawcett. This was not only a sentimental gesture (in the best sense of the word) but a fruitful means of fund-raising, as the Mary Stott Appeal was much more effective than a general appeal, just as in the 1930s it was much easier to raise money for the Millicent Fawcett Hall than for the Women's Service Hall.

Buildings – their importance to Fawcett in particular and women's organisations in general

First and foremost, women's organisations need decent premises as much as anyone else, as long as these building enhance rather than distract from their core purpose Women's groups are usually poor and for too long they have had to put up with very tatty and inadequate premises – the equivalent of 'dangerous oilcloth on the stairs' from 1881 or the intimidating walk to Harleyford Road in the 1980s. But do they need large historic buildings? I think the answer is that they only need them if they can afford them and they come really well endowed (as gifts to the National Trust have to be).

That Sarah Clegg paid for Women's Service House, the building of the Millicent Fawcett Hall and the rest of the complex was wonderful for the Society – it raised their profile, their morale, brought in new members, made all sorts of things possible. But once she died intestate the financial worries started and got worse and worse. As Virgina Woolf said, 'a woman must have money and a room of her own' and that is just as true of rooms in the plural.

The fact that so many people gave so much time, energy and in some cases money, to save these buildings testifies to how important they are – and always will be – to the women's movement. But reacquiring them in the difficult 1990s would have needed a completely different set of skills to running an effective campaigning organisation – it is not an easy matter (if not impossible) to combine the two.[27] So in the end for Westminster School to acquire this site (especially now it has young women as students) and give access to the women's movement was probably the best outcome all round. It is a pity the Hall itself is swathed in black curtains because it is used as a drama studio. But at least it is still there and accessible as a permanent reminder of a key period in the women's movement.

THE WOMEN'S SERVICE TRUST AND CHARITABLE STATUS

The Women's Service Trust (WST) has reverberated down the years of Fawcett's history from 1926 to 1988, during which it was its financial lifeline.

The story started in 1924 when the Society was at a low ebb and a supporter, Sarah Clegg, gave it £1,000 which allowed it to move out of a small room in Victoria into comparatively palatial premises in Marsham Street in Westminster. When Sarah Clegg decided to give more money she set up a trust to do this, with the aim of promoting 'the equality of women with men in political and economic opportunity'. The WST was to continue in existence until twenty-one years after the death of the last surviving trustee – the three trustees being Philippa Strachey, Edith Glover and Sarah Clegg herself. This allowed the Society to embark on constructing the Millicent Fawcett Hall and other buildings between Marsham and Tufton streets.

> The Trust was created because Miss Clegg did not want the Society to own the properties which she gradually acquired in case they at any time changed their aims and objects – which accounts for the wording of the Trust which allows the Trustees to give the income and capital to any other body with the same objects in the event of the Society not following the original objectives of the Trust or if the Society could be said to have fulfilled its objects.[1]

In 1930 Sarah Clegg died intestate. This involved the Trust in some death duties before her plan for the buildings was completed and it was left to the Trustees to find the money to finish construction. The bank allowed an overdraft, the total of which, £6,000, was paid off by Philippa Fawcett in 1939.

The Marsham Street buildings were eventually sold to Westminster City Council and 27 Wilfred Street bought in 1957:

> The WST derives its income from the interests on the investment of the money received from the sale of the Marsham Street property less the cost of the purchase of 27 Wilfred Street. It soon became obvious that the income was not sufficient to cover the needs of the Society and the Library and in consequence in 1957 the Fawcett Library Trust was formed, with charitable status and the Women's Service Library in its care. This enabled arrangements to be made for the income from the WST to be covenanted by the Society in sufficient amount to cover the rates and other common facilities.

However the WST was only producing £2,500 per annum (since its income came only from investments, membership and legacies with no fundraising). This meant the Society continued to live on a shoestring as its income was never sufficient to meet the bare running costs, leaving no room for expansion of activities. A further crisis developed in the 1970s with the possibility of capital gains being liable, and there were plans to sell 27 Wilfred Street and find a separate home for the Library. In 1974 the Trustees of the WST sought Counsel's advice on the validity of the Trust and were told that the Trust was 'unenforceable and void' and advised that the Trustees would be at personal risk if they applied the money, either capital or income. In October, Counsel further advised that the Trustees should take the matter to court.

There followed a time of both intense anxiety and poverty for the Society, with payments frozen and activity further curtailed. On 26 February 1976 the court case was at last heard and the Trust declared 'valid and charitable' and eventually entered in the Central Register of Charities. This was a great victory not just for the Society but for equality for women generally. The Society was now back in business, and 27 Wilfred Street could be sold.

The next landmark came in 1988, twenty-one years after the death of Philippa Strachey, the last survivor of the original trustees of 1926. This led to the dissolution of the Women's Service Trust and the establishment of the Fawcett Trust so as to be able to maximise the tax advantages of charitable status for income earned from the assets of the Society and on funds raised for charitable work. A capital sum (£265,000 in 1994) was moved from the Women's Service Trust to the Fawcett Trust. The chair of Trustees was Sandy Shulman, who had been chair of the Society for two years. There were searching discussions about the relationship between the Society and the Trust, a realisation that the Society could no longer live on investments alone and of the need for the Trust to fundraise if the Society were to grow. Conservative members of the society questioned whether the Society needed to grow at all and found even four members of staff too many. But in fact Fawcett's income improved immeasurably:

	Income excluding Trust	*with Fawcett Trust*
1987	£10,500	£42,000
1994	£91,000	£120,000

In 2002, after a rather tortuous process that had been running since 1997, Fawcett became incorporated – i.e. a company limited by guarantee – and in 2005, after much legal advice and two unsuccessful attempts since 1984 it also became a charity. This would bring considerable benefits that included gift aid on donations and access to a wider range of funding streams and to charitable rates on products and services. This advantage became possible with the new guidelines on campaigning and necessitated a re-wording of Item 3 of Fawcett's Memorandum of Association to read:

To promote equality and diversity, in particular equality between women and men, and to eliminate gender discrimination for the benefit of the public by:

a) Raising awareness of all aspects of discrimination in society by publications, lectures, use of the media, public advocacy and other means of communication;
b) Conducting or commissioning research on equality and publishing the results of the same to the public;
c) Advancing education in equality and diversity whether by teaching or producing materials;
d) Promoting attitudes, customs and practices in favour of equality by the use of publications, media and public advocacy.

Fawcett reckoned that adopting these objects would not seriously limit its work, although it would need to remain in 'constructive dialogue' with the Charitable Commissioners. On 7 March 2005 it held an Extraordinary General Meeting to approve the changes to the constitution before going forward to register as a charity. (This was, ironically, the same occasion on which the Society launched a new report *Money, Money, Money: Is it still a rich man's world?*, a state-of-the-nation report on women's employment, pay, income and pensions.) Once charitable status was achieved, Fawcett was then able to dissolve the Fawcett Trust, which had in effect acted as its charitable arm.

Sandy Shulman, a trustee throughout the life of the Fawcett Trust and its longest-serving chair, remembered

> the excitement generated by the WST funds being passed to the Fawcett Trust; there were many suggestions how best the money could be used, some very constructive, others wild and woolly. I was deeply conscious that the trustees had to ensure the funds weren't frittered away or used by the Society for non-charitable purposes. Our aim was to help Fawcett sustain and grow its reputation and membership through campaigns and research and also to attract funding from other charities. I believe with the help and work of the Fawcett Trust the Society was able to fulfill a dream: to feel secure and flourish and not slip backwards into the old hand to mouth ways. Once the Society achieved charitable status there was no need for the Fawcett Trust and I know the trustees applauded while heaving a huge sigh of relief.2

Chapter 6

'You have won rooms of your own in the house hitherto exclusively owned by men': the glory days of the Junior Council

These words were spoken by Virginia Woolf as part of her lecture on 'Professions for women' on 21 January 1931 in the Millicent Fawcett Hall as she looked out over her glittering audience. She went on to remind the women assembled there that they must pay the rent and tenant the rooms (see Chapter 5, page 70).

By then, the Junior Council (JC) was already five years old. It had been formed at a meeting of young women of the London and National Society for Women's Service (LNSWS) on 28 June 1926. At its next meeting on 28 September an Executive Committee was elected. The Council emerged partly out of the passing of the Sex Disqualification (Removal) Act of 1919, which had left women who were entering professions newly open to them isolated without the opportunities and networks available to men. The first party (of many – the Junior Council always agreed about having fun as well as serious campaigning) was held on 15 December. By the first Annual Meeting on 3 May 1927 the membership had risen from fifteen to 175, and they were compiling a register of activities of women in London. In its first Annual Report, produced in June 1927, the Council was eloquent both in thanking the LNSWS for 'experience and subtle encouragement' and in confidently declaring: 'There is no limit to the activity of the Junior Council. May we convince the outside world that wisdom is no longer synonymous with age and that youth and judgement are no longer incompatible.'[1] The report went on to explain how the JC had been born out of a 'great need for an organisation that would bring together young professional and business women and students and would help them to overcome the obstacles which still lie in the way of those who during recent years have entered professional and business life'. The Junior Council kept unswervingly to this aim. From the outset, moreover, it made a point of including women students in its activities, inviting them to meet young women already profes-

**LONDON & NATIONAL
SOCIETY FOR WOMEN'S SERVICE**
THE JUNIOR COUNCIL

invites

to a party
in *WOMEN'S SERVICE HALL*
Entrance by 27, Marsham Street, Westminster
or 46, Tufton Street,

on *Wednesday, 21st January, 1931, at 8 p.m.*
DAME ETHEL SMYTH & VIRGINIA WOOLF
will be the Guests of the Evening and will speak on
MUSIC AND LITERATURE

*R.S.V.P. to the Secretary, Junior Council,
27, Marsham Street, Westminster, S.W. 1.*

Morning Dress.

sionally active and organising meetings with speakers at women's colleges.

The JC's origins were recalled again eight years later in the Annual Report of 1935:

> The Junior Society is now nine years old, and is as vigorous and essentially young as when it was first founded It is clearly proved that the mixture of purpose and entertainment which it provides meets a real need, and its ninth birthday may be a suitable moment to recall how and why the Junior Council came into existence and to state the reason for its continued success.
>
> The London and National Society for Women's Service has been in existence since 1866 and has passed through many evolutions. After working for the vote it turned its energies towards improving the economic position of women and by 1926 it seemed that the young women enjoying the opportunities and freedom already gained should be drawn in to share in the work that remained to be done. But somehow they were not interested. They definitely disliked the idea of 'feminism', knew nothing of the pre-war difficulties of women, and thought the world lay open to them without any special disabilities attaching to themselves as women.
>
> The Executive Committee saw all this and were troubled by it. They knew that there was still a great deal of work to be done before professions and businesses lay open to men and women on equal terms, and that those who could do that work were the young women themselves. So they decided to try and form a Junior Branch.
>
> Warned by the experiences of other societies they decided that a mere Junior Branch would not be attractive so they offered real independence to their proposed Junior Council and did not even lay down any rights or conditions of membership.

35. Invitation to a joint talk by Virginia Woolf and Dame Ethel Smyth, 21 January 1931

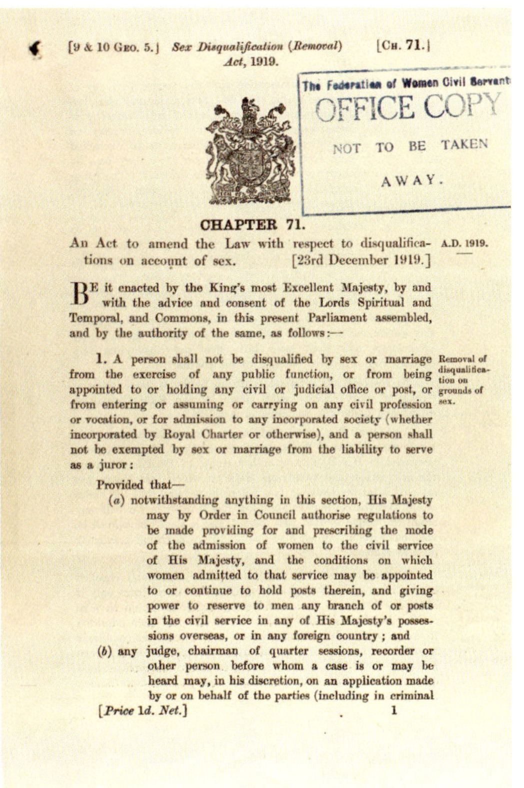

[9 & 10 GEO. 5.] *Sex Disqualification (Removal)* [CH. 71.]
Act, 1919.

CHAPTER 71.

An Act to amend the Law with respect to disqualifica- A.D. 1919.
tions on account of sex. [23rd December 1919.]

BE it enacted by the King's most Excellent Majesty, by and
with the advice and consent of the Lords Spiritual and
Temporal, and Commons, in this present Parliament assembled,
and by the authority of the same, as follows :—

1. A person shall not be disqualified by sex or marriage *Removal of*
from the exercise of any public function, or from being *disqualifica-tion on*
appointed to or holding any civil or judicial office or post, or *grounds of*
from entering or assuming or carrying on any civil profession *sex.*
or vocation, or for admission to any incorporated society (whether
incorporated by Royal Charter or otherwise), and a person shall
not be exempted by sex or marriage from the liability to serve
as a juror :

Provided that—
(*a*) notwithstanding anything in this section, His Majesty
may by Order in Council authorise regulations to
be made providing for and prescribing the mode
of the admission of women to the civil service
of His Majesty, and the conditions on which
women admitted to that service may be appointed
to or continue to hold posts therein, and giving
power to reserve to men any branch of or posts
in the civil service in any of His Majesty's posses-
sions overseas, or in any foreign country ; and
(*b*) any judge, chairman of quarter sessions, recorder or
other person before whom a case is or may be
heard may, in his discretion, on an application made
by or on behalf of the parties (including in criminal

[*Price* 1*d. Net.*] 1

36. Sex Disqualification (Removal) Act, 1919

They invited twenty-three young women to meet and discuss the project and offered them premises, money for organisation and a free hand. Then they stood back and left them to it.

The Junior Council took on the challenge and developed according to its own ideas. After a year it voluntarily adopted the same objects as the Society and accepted the proposal that membership of the Junior Council should automatically carry with it membership of the Society. It developed its scheme of monthly parties, its recreational side, and subsequently its Group system, and at every stage has taken its own decisions and managed its own affairs.[2]

From its earliest days the JC was very activity based and these activities not only brought in existing members but were very effective in recruiting new ones. On 28 June 1927 a meeting at 35 Marsham Street on 'Opportunities in the department stores' and 'Women in the Civil Service' attracted an audience of seventy and brought it eleven new members. On 24 November of the same year, a talk on 'Should married women work?', with Dora Russell as one of the speakers, led to a lively debate, ninety in attendance and nine new members.

The JC was also good at organising celebrations and honouring the achievements of its members. The Annual Report for 1928, for instance, describes how its year ended 'with a blaze of glory' with a party on 10 March for Elizabeth Scott, a long-time member and architect-elect of the Shakespeare Memorial Theatre in Stratford. For thirteen years, from 1926 to 1939, this pattern of busy activity, sustained socialising and creative initiatives marked the existence of the Junior Council and is reflected in its annual reports.[3] The Council and its groups were able to attract eminent speakers and acknowledged experts for their gatherings, a measure of the JC's appeal as a forum. Some of the names of speakers resonate to this day and meetings were quite frequently written up in the press. (A detailed list of the Junior Council's parties and talks appears at Appendix 1.)

By 1929, the Junior Council 'was enlarging its activities in all directions', as it announced in its third Annual Report.[4] The formation of the Speakers' Class in 1928, designed to give members practice in public speaking, led directly to the setting up of the Debating Society with, even at that stage, sixty-seven members. Some of them were asked by the BBC to discuss the subject 'Is the vote worth having?' The Society proceeded to debate three more very challenging subjects in 1928: in July, 'A belief in one-self is better than a bank balance'; in October, 'That legal sanction be given to trial marriage', and in November, with two outside speakers brought in, 'That the hope of the world lies in fascism rather than socialism' (the motion was defeated). There was time for two more debates before the Annual Meeting: in February 1929, 'That the term politician is synonymous with humbug', and in March a debate between ten members of the Club and the 1919 Club on the subject 'That premeditation is more common in female than in male criminals'.

The Junior Council continued to hold regular parties with speakers, preceded by dinner for forty or fifty guests (organised by the Social Sub-Committee). Subjects included 'The future of women in public life and industry' and 'American labour legislation as affecting women and children'. What amounted to a seminar on 'Openings in science for women today' in December 1928 had seven speakers and a very large attendance (including students from seven London colleges). In January 1929 a series of parties on the forthcoming general election was inaugurated, at one of which Nancy Astor spoke with enthusiasm and delight about the young women of today – and out of the interest generated by this came the setting up of a Political Sub-Committee. Once formed, this group decided that its two main lobbying points at the election were to be, firstly, equal pay for equal work in the Civil Service and secondly, the removal of the marriage bar for women employed by the central and local authorities.

The 1929 report ended on a high. Membership of the JC had risen to 370. Now that their offices had moved to the splendid new building down the road at number 27 Marsham Street, the upper floors of 35 Marsham Street (The Fleece) could be converted into 'charmingly designed' bedrooms and a sitting room for the use of JC members. A Publicity Sub-Committee ensured that the activities and facilities of the Junior Council were widely known but members were also encouraged to spread the word.

> The success of the Junior Council is obvious. The measure of success it can attain for its aims and objects depends upon its strength and this in turn upon every individual member.
>
> The Committee begs you to make known the Junior Council to all your friends, to stimulate their interest by bringing them to the monthly parties; and to register a vow to introduce at least one new member this year.

One marked and impressive aspect of the Junior Council was the warmth of feeling between it and the main Society, characterised by mutual respect, gratitude and support. This included the Society's president, Dame Millicent Fawcett, to whom the JC

37. Junior Council, Report for 1929

took a delegation in early autumn 1928 'to thank her warmly for the great work she and others of her age have done towards the achievement for women'.[5] Millicent was in the last year of her life (she died in August 1929) but as committed to the cause of young women as ever and she responded with enormous enthusiasm, telling them they were 'the very embodiment of our dreams'. In what was in effect both a call to action and a handing on of the baton, she wrote:

> It is very splendid to see you taking up your responsibilities and carrying on our work into the new fields where it must now be pursued…I look upon the formation of your Council and its achievements with the greatest pride, and I feel that the future of the movement will be safe and triumphant in your hands. I believe, of course, that it will change and develop; you will probably find new methods and new needs, and your ways will be the ways of full citizens instead of the way of beggars and outcasts as ours for so long had to be. But I feel confident that you will find, as we did, that the cause of the real freedom of women is a great one, worth one's best service, and that you will never lose sight of it even amidst your new opportunities.
>
> It is not the only good cause in the world, nor the only one you will care for. But it does lie with you to care for it; and for all its changes it is the same as that which we older women cared for. And it does lie close to our hands, as women, and it must not be forgotten until it is wholly achieved. You know from your own experience that equal pay and equal economic opportunities are still withheld from us.
>
> I shall expect to see you individually and collectively putting your shoulders to that wheel and pushing the car of progress along in your generation as we tried to do in ours; and I know you will find that, in this struggle, there is enjoyment, pleasure and real interest as long as you believe in your cause and in your associates. And I am firmly convinced that justice and freedom for women are things worth securing not only for their own sakes, but for civilization itself.
>
> Believe me, with warm interest and great expectations
>
> Yours sincerely
>
> M. G. Fawcett[6]

The Junior Council continued to live up to the promise she had seen in them. It placed great emphasis on assisting its members into various professions and on arranging for prominent women to come and talk about their careers, from insurance ('What at first glance seemed a very dull and dreary subject, on closer inspection became a truly romantic and enthralling matter'[7]), to the probation service, property management and the legal profession.

The Junior Council entered the 1930s on a high note. The Annual Meeting on 24 April 1931 was the first to be held in the new building and showed them 'united in their determination to strive for equal pay for equal work'.[8] Members were urged to become involved in local government and a study circle and series of lectures was suggested to facilitate this work. The 1931 Annual Report gives more detail. Membership is up to nearly 600, all of whom are prepared to see that the 'opportunities fought for by the Society in its earlier days are enjoyed and made use of to the full'. There is strong recognition of the difference which the move to the new premises has made:

The gift of the Society's present freehold premises by Miss Sarah Clegg has undoubtedly vastly contributed to the rapid development of the Junior Council, which, without such facilities, must have had to restrict the scope of its work.[9]

There had been a range of interesting speakers, including Lilian Baylis on the Old Vic, Sir Samuel Hoare on 'The development of civil aviation and women's part in it' (very well attended) and Mr Stobart and Miss Mary Somerville on 'The serious uses of broadcasting' – education and school broadcasting. There were meetings on women in commerce, in manufacturing, in retail, in advertising and in publishing. The most renowned speakers of all were the famous duo of Ethel Smyth and Virginia Woolf, discussing music and literature on 21 January 1931 (see Chapter 5). The Debating Society went from strength to strength. Additional clubs were also set up in this period – a Swimming Club, which met in the Great Smith Street Baths, and a Walkers' Club, which met on alternate Sundays and was very popular.

The following year the opening of Elizabeth Scott's Shakespeare theatre in Stratford-upon-Avon was noted in the proceedings of the Annual Meeting on 27 April 1932, which also observed that the facilities in the 'Members' Centre' in the new building, although much improved, could not really be equivalent to the services of a club, which would cost much more.

Resolutions passed at the Annual Meeting concerned the setting up of six special groups – on art, science, law, social work, commerce and politics – to provide greater opportunity for the discussion of professional and business life between members. Each group would have a president and a secretary and would function under the control of the Junior Council Committee and when public action was contemplated, under the Executive Committee of the Society. Among other initiatives, the Amateur Dramatic Society was up and running and the just formed Junior Council Orchestra was tuning up to play at an At Home to be given for women MPs on 29 April.

The Annual Report for 1932 noted a celebration dinner for Irene Ward, a JC member, on her election to Parliament as Conservative member for Wallsend. A meeting on housing, chaired by Elizabeth Scott, focused on the need for building houses at a rental which the poorest members of the population could afford to pay (social housing by another name). Evening parties with speakers continued. The Debating Society had a successful year with eight meetings. In an intimation of the gathering storm ahead, on 19 June 1931, JC members were invited to hear Philip Noel Baker MP propose 'That it should be possible at the forthcoming Disarmament Conference to achieve a general limitation of armaments, which will materially contribute to the greater security of nations'. In a further debate, the motion 'That Russia in architecture, as in other directions, is leading the world' was proposed by the architect Clough Williams Ellis but was defeated. On 12 February 1932, the Junior Council and senior members of the Society (led by Ray Strachey and the Hon. Mrs Spencer Graves) debated the motion 'That it is better to be old than young' (carried by a large majority). In speaking to the report to the 1932 Annual Meeting, Philippa Strachey picked up on the subject of this debate and had this to say:

> Everyone knows the proverb 'si jeunesse savait, si vieillesse pouvait.' The Society is nearly seventy years of age, so may perhaps be considered to be old – though not, I hope, stick-in-the mud old. The Junior Council is about five years of age, so may perhaps be considered to be young, although not, I hope, callow young. I cannot help believing that these two together may be able to find a way of defeating the proverb and combining the 'savvy' of the old with the energies of the young. Looking back over the past five years,...no one can deny that the Junior Council has brought fresh strength into the Society, firstly, by advertising it and increasing the membership, and secondly, by generally cheering it up and giving good friends good reason to act as benefactors.[10]

However the benefactors did not prevent the need for the House Membership subscriptions to be raised from 7/6 to 10/- .

The year 1931-32 ended on an extremely optimistic note:

> If the enthusiasm of such women coupled with the work of the pioneers of the Suffrage movement, is sustained in the Junior Council, no limit can be placed upon the importance it may ultimately assume in the sphere of women's work.[11]

At its seventh Annual Meeting in 1933 membership of the JC was reported to have risen to 641, encompassing 117 different occupations. The opening of Elizabeth Scott's Memorial Theatre in Stratford-upon-Avon was an occasion for congratulation. The special groups set up at the previous Annual Meeting were in full swing and 'proving their value as a means of promoting increased cooperation between members and of affording greater opportunities for the discussion of questions related to the professions and occupations represented'. The Law Group, for instance, discussed 'Opening the legal profession to women' and the Science Group 'Openings in science for women to-day'. At two memorable parties, Sir Arthur Salter spoke on 'What the forthcoming World Conferences can do for recovery', and two well-known journalists, Hubert Griffith and H.W. Smith, on a recent visit to Russia. Both talks were written up in the press. The Debating Society continued in force with the proposal 'That modern fiction is out of touch with modern life', chaired by the novelist Storm Jameson. The Amateur Dramatic Society, which had changed its name to The Marsham Street Players, produced three one-act plays in December 1932. The Swimming and Walking Clubs continued to give a lot of pleasure, and the Junior Council was said to be closely in touch with the League of Nations.

All this was very exciting and encouraging, but the 1933 Annual Report ends on a rather ominous note, in relation to both the Senior and the Junior section of the Society:

> Since the end of 1930, the Executive Committee of the Society has been oppressed by financial anxieties and it became evident in December last that if the work of the Society is to continue, a special effort would have to be made to establish the finances of the Society on a more satisfactory and permanent basis.

To this end a special campaign was inaugurated at the beginning of this year and a Membership Campaign Committee, including Senior and Junior members, was set up which organised a variety of meetings and entertainments to stimulate outside interest in the work of the Society, and, by enlarging membership, to secure a steady income.[12]

Financial anxieties were not of course new, and they were not getting better.

Things still seemed buoyant in 1934 – 'a very full year of development in various directions and in the extension of membership both in numbers and representative occupations', as the year's Annual Report announced.[13] Meetings on 'many varied subjects' were organised both by the groups and more centrally. In March the historian G. P. Gooch spoke on 'Dictatorships in Central Europe' and 'sent us away with a much keener grasp of the international situation in Europe'[14] The Law Group held a 'Moot', a book discussion and, rather surprisingly, a dance. The Political Group organised a study circle on 'Indian women's franchise' and took part with the Debating Society in a debate on 'Is democratic government worth preserving?' – resulting in a vote in favour of democracy. The Science Group held meetings on 'Women's work in astronomy', 'The capture and training of elephants in India' (very popular), organised a visit to the General Post Office at Mount Pleasant and arranged a 'Frivolous Party' with games, competitions and prizes – judged a 'complete success'. The Social Work Group met a number of times to discuss different aspects of social work. The Marsham Street Players read and performed various plays. The only blot on this horizon of success was the winding-up of the Debating Club 'owing to recent lack of interest'. It is not clear whether its demise was due to the new opportunities offered by the other groups.

On a more positive note the Executive Committee announced the formation of a Women's Employment Federation housed in LNSWS premises at 31 Marsham Street. This was intended 'to act as a clearing house to which organisations which specialise in … the employment of educated women, can contribute the varied information and experience'.[15] The Junior Council was one of thirty-one organisations to join the Federation, an example of collaborative working which characterises Fawcett's work till today.

By 1935, 'foreign politics and international affairs' were figuring largely in the programmes of the Junior Council. Professor Harold Laski and Major Yeats-Brown debated the motion 'Fascism is incompatible with free speech' to a packed hall that included a number of fascists. 'Following this, a questionnaire was drawn up on the position to be given to women in the proposed Fascist State: this was sent to the Fascist Headquarters and received a full and detailed reply'.[16] Sir Norman Angell spoke on 'Pacifism and national defence', Geoffrey Crowther on 'Britain – the pharisee?' and Horsfall Carter on 'The Saar Force and its significance'. And in a very crowded meeting, Lord Lothian discussed 'Proposals for constitutional changes in India'. Back on the home front, Miss E. A. Ford spoke on 'Equal pay – ought we to have it and how can we get it', showing how inequality of pay is not only 'essentially unfair' but also leads to 'blackleg labour'. On the social side of the JC's programme, quarterly sherry parties were introduced so that new members could meet the Executive Committee and offi-

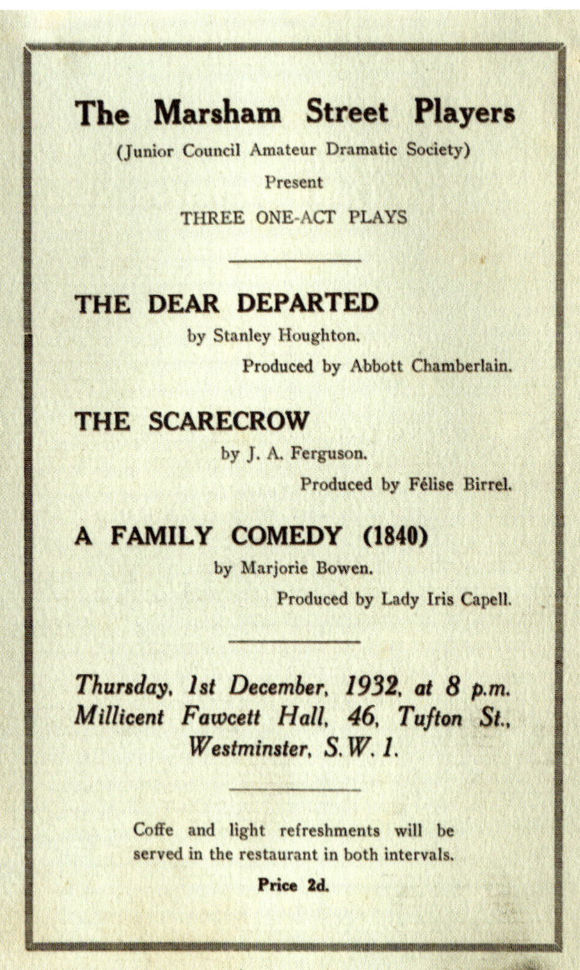

38. Marsham Street Players programme, 1932

cials of the groups. The latter continued to hold multiple events, ranging over the arts, commerce, business, careers, legal matters and politics. In February 1935, Dr Hugh Dalton spoke on 'Foreign dictatorships and the danger of war', and there was an informal discussion on the conversations held between H. G. Wells and Stalin in Moscow, with copies of the Wells-Stalin pamphlet available. The Science Group organised meetings and an outing to the wildlife sanctuary at Wicken Fen. The Social Work Group hosted meetings on 'Housing schemes on the continent and in England' and on camps for unemployed men.

The Walkers' Club had a particularly exciting time, with an all-night ramble around London in two separate groups, one group visiting the BBC, the *Daily Telegraph*, Clerkenwell Telephone Exchange, the GPO and the Gas Light and Coke Co.'s premises at Nine Elms, finishing at Covent Garden at 6 am and then to Women's Service House for breakfast. The other group took in Battersea Power Station, the *Times*, and the London Wholesale Dairies at Vauxhall. The Swimming Club continued its vigorous trajectory. The Marsham Street Players had a mixed year. Their first production of two one-act plays was not well attended and actually lost money, but when the second of these was entered in the Drama League Festival it did very well. And Millicent Fawcett Hall was practically full for the second production (*The Distaff Side* by John van Druten) in March 1935, which produced a profit. Nonetheless, the Group was sufficiently concerned about its audiences to inaugurate a scheme of Subscriber Membership, each subscriber paying ten shillings a year and receiving two seats for each show.

The Junior Council continued to be actively concerned with the Public Work Sub-Committee run by the Executive of the main Society which, as explained in the 1935 Annual Report,

keeps a constant watch over the interests of women, particularly in regard to matters affecting their economic position. This Committee has been actively occupied during the year with the appointment of women in posts in various Government Departments, e.g., the Board of Education, the Home Office, the

> Ministry of Transport and the Unemployed Assistance Board; with the opening of the Diplomatic and Consular Services to women; with the employment of women police; with the position of married women as regards employment, nationality rights and legal status generally; with the working of the Shop Acts, and with other such matters. It has taken part in the stand of British women for the Indian Women's Franchise, it has followed the position of women in Germany and has joined in the international movement for raising the status of women through the League of Nations. It has worked also in various ways towards the goal of equal pay for equal work and towards obtaining for women in industry an approach to that measure of free opportunity which has been won by women in the professions.[17]

This is a massive testament not only to the Junior Council but to the work of the London and National Society for Women's Service as a whole.

An audit of what the Junior Council had achieved so far is given in the Annual Report of 1936. It

> furnishes the reply to those who ask 'What is the good of the Junior Council?' To questioners who assume that no disabilities remain for women, the Junior Council retorts: 'Do they get equal pay with men? Are all women free to continue their work after marriage? Can they enter the Consular and Diplomatic Service?'
>
> In each case the answer is in the negative!
>
> The last eighteen years since the passing of the Sex Disqualification Removal Act, have given so many opportunities to women, that it is all too easy to take what is there and to ignore the obstacles which still exist, unless they affect us personally. It is only then we realise the need for a well-informed and authoritative body in a position to take effective action. There is also another side which is of equal value to business and professional women. It is the opportunity they have of meeting and getting to know others in different spheres of work, whose knowledge may be of inestimable value…[18]

The report showed fewer meetings during the course of the year. Amongst events which did take place was an extremely well attended talk on 'The trial of Sir Thomas More' and an evening 'Behind the screens' on the history of cinema. Another talk examined 'How the Swedish women reached their present position'. The Arts and Letters Group hosted an evening of Jacobite songs and visited Sir Herbert Cook's art collection at Doughty House at Richmond. The Law Group held their annual fixture with the 1919 Club on the 'eminently topical subject' 'That this House welcomes Belisha as a worthy follower of Hitler'. After a heated debate, the motion was lost by three votes. Another topical discussion was of 'Legal and commercial effects of economic sanctions', chaired by the 'apostle of peace', Hilda Clark. The chair of the Law Group, Miss Irene Stoney, instituted readings from books in the Library once a month 'with a view to familiarising members with the many unknown treasures on its shelves', starting with *The Trial of Mary Blandy* in February 1752.

The Political Group held 'one of the pleasantest parties' given for secretaries to MPs, which brought 'a number of valuable members to the Junior Council'. Just before

Christmas 1935, the Group constituted itself as an Inter-party Congress, which disclosed existing abuses in the selection of parliamentary candidates, and suggested the best methods for securing youth representation. A 'special welcome was extended to hecklers and agitators, but in actual fact the discussion was kept on an amicable and amusing plane'.[19] The Science Group organised meetings and expeditions. Two groups, however, the Commerce and Business Group and the Social Work Group, proved to be on their last legs through lack of interest and insufficient support, and wound up their activities.

More cheerfully there were several sherry parties, at one of which Miss Arnot Robertson spoke on the theme 'That women won't be freed', to which Ray Strachey replied vigorously. The Junior Council was represented on the Women's Advisory Council of the League of Nations Union. The recently formed Bridge Circle met every week. The Marsham Street Players had three performances, came eleventh out of ninety in the Drama League Festival and acquired an interior set of scenery which could be let out to other drama societies, thus providing a useful source of income

The Annual Report 1936 ended with an analysis of the work of the Society as a whole as well as of the Junior Council within it:

> The Junior Council participates in the Society's general work in two ways. In the first place, its members, equally with the other members of the Society, are eligible for the main Executive Committee, and of the fifteen members of that body five are, this year, members of the Junior Council; one of whom holds the distinguished position of Chairman of the Society's Executive Committee. In the second place members of the Junior Council take part in the general work through membership of the Executive's Public Work Sub-Committee which meets monthly to consider matters affecting those interests of women which come within the Society's scope.[20]

These interests, outlined in the 1935 Annual Report (see above), continued the same.

Financial problems are a theme of the Annual Meeting in April 1937, the situation giving rise to so 'much anxiety' that it was 'proposed to issue a special appeal for a donation of 5/- by each member, which will free the Junior Council from this burden for three years, if everyone contributes.'[21] At this meeting we first see Kathleen Halpin, elected as honorary secretary, who was to become such a prominent part of the life of the wider Society , right up to the attempt to save the Millicent Fawcett Hall in the 1990s (see Chapter 5), when she was ninety-five. Miss Halpin opened discussions on how to attract more younger members by setting up student groups, 'since those who belonged to the Junior Council at its inception eleven years ago are no longer very ìjunior"'.[22] It was suggested articled clerks and girls apprenticed to various professions might be added to this category.

The Annual Report for 1937 welcomed over a hundred new members but still urged existing members to persuade their friends to join. The Groups co-operated on a number of monthly parties – including literary parties on 'Children's reading down the ages' chaired by Noel Streatfeild, Walter de la Mare on 'Lewis Carroll and nonsense', and Dorothy Sayers speaking on the provocative subject 'Are women human?' Marcel

Boulestin spoke on 'French vs English food', John Walker from Thomas Cook on travel in Switzerland and the Black Forest, and Lawrence Wingfield on the development of civil aviation. The Science Group organised a talk on 'Air raid precautions': 'how each one could do their part in protecting the civilian population in case of raids'. There was a meeting on 'Rhythmic exercise', followed by a regular class in the Hall, regular bridge events and even a chamber music concert. This was much enjoyed but there was a worrying note about the financial implications:

> But unless every seat in the Hall is sold it is not possible to cover the expenses and on this occasion, good as the programme was, the Hall was not full and if more concerts are to be organised, as so many members would like, a certain numbers of guarantors will have to be found.[23]

The Walkers' Club had instituted a longer walk over the Whitsun holiday weekend. The club continued its regular Sunday walks including on occasion joining a ramblers' excursion train, 'thus enabling them to go further afield', while the Marsham Street Players finished their season with a cocktail party for all the men who had taken part during the year. 'It should be mentioned that men are not full members … but are invited to take part by the Players'.[24] The Players had been earning much-needed money by letting their scenery to several dramatic societies who used the Millicent Fawcett Hall. Their report ended on a slightly disconsolate note, hoping for 'a more lively interest by the senior members of the Society and the Junior Council' and soliciting their 'active support'.[25]

The Annual Report concluded with a recognition of the Junior Council's active involvement in the Public Work Committee and of their meetings with the Executive of the main Society to discuss the internal organisation of the Society, 'with a view to clarifying the present function of the JC and determining a direction for its future policy'.[26]

The Annual Report for 1938 celebrates the Coronation but also strikes a note of foreboding: 'Today democracy is being challenged on all sides and reactionary principles have triumphed in countries which were the first to give emancipation to women...' The Junior Council goes on to express its support for the Society's project to endow the Library, its 'one great possession', seeing in that a kind of bulwark against 'any retrogressive influences that may creep in in the future'.[27]

Monthly parties with speakers continued, among them an extremely well attended talk on 'Life on a farm in South Russia' and 'one of the most delightful parties the Junior Council has ever had' when Dr L. D. A. Hussey spoke on his journeys with Shackleton in the Antarctic in 1914-16. The importance of the groups was reiterated: 'they fulfil one of the principal objects of the Junior Council by providing opportunities for members to meet and exchange views on their own works as well as topical subjects. These small informal gatherings encourage individual expression of an opinion in a way which is not possible at larger meetings.'[28] Their outings, talks and debates were varied, topical and imaginative. The Law Group, for instance, held a party in the Library where they read from unpublished family letters, another on the alterations brought about by the Matrimonial Causes Act, and were busy planning meetings on 'Voluntary euthanasia' and 'Penal reform'. The Science Group hosted a discussion on 'Modern architecture in relation to modern life', where they voted 'by an overwhelming majority in favour of present day design in Architecture and Furnishing'. The Marsham Street Players spent much of the year preparing for the very successful and ambitious production of *Lady Precious Stream* which had two performances, rather than just one, in April 1938. They also began the year with a balance in hand and as a result were able to spend £15 on stage lighting in the Hall (money not well spent when we consider what was to happen to the Hall within the next few years). The Bridge Circle instituted a small class for beginners partly organised by Miss Douie (moonlighting from the Library!). Finally a new group, the Twenties Group, was formed to try and bring in younger members to the Junior Council, with events like card parties, badminton games and so on. The conclusion was that this was not successful despite there being a real need for such a group.

Meanwhile, officers of the JC's Executive and individual groups continued to be involved with the Public Work Committee of the Society on issues such as the Ministry of Labour's 'Cost of living enquiry' and an ad hoc committee, chaired by Philippa Strachey, to enquire into the position of salaried architects in government and county council departments. The Public Work Committee was recognised as the 'principal fount of knowledge on the work upon which the Society is engaged'.

The Junior Council's Annual Report for 1939 proved to be its final one. It describes a familiar list of parties and speakers: on China, on 'Penal reform', on Palestine, on 'The witch cult' and, by the founder of the Windmill Theatre, on 'Why should non-stop ever stop?' At one of the recently instituted sherry parties, the chair of the Women's Voluntary Services spoke on the work of her organisation and the need for wholehearted co-operation from business and professional women, and at another 'The work of women housing managers' was the topic. The Political Group organised discussions on pensions and work conditions. More sombrely, they invited Dame Rachel Crowdy to discuss 'Should women be conscripted in time of war?' and to argue 'the vital importance of a proper organisation of women power for the service of the nation'. The Arts and Letters Group focused on recent discoveries and work at Westminster Abbey. They also instituted 'Finger and fork suppers' after the sherry parties so that members could get to know each other better.

If all this sounds, in 1939, a little like fiddling while Rome begins to burn, the Opening Remarks to the Report stress the full seriousness of the situation:

> Abroad we see the lights of freedom going out one by one and this year has seen two more countries losing their independence and suppressing their women's organisations' with the subsequent curtailment of individual freedom.
>
> All this makes it clear that our work for the future must be to see that we are prepared to play our part in maintaining the democratic ideals and principles which are the very essence of our civilisation. Realising as we must that the nation's reserve of strength lies in its women, the second thing with which we should vitally concern ourselves is the part to be played by women in the organisation of the nation to meet the dangers which threaten us…

The Junior Council was determined to contribute to this effort via the Women's Voluntary Services while still maintaining their original mission 'to safeguard and improve the position of women in business and the professions'.[29] Yet they were sufficiently confident in their future to produce an amended constitution in 1939, after a whole series of attempts to do so since 1930.

It is at this stage that the Junior Council, thirteen years old, vibrant, involved, committed, more or less disappears from view. There are occasional references to meetings of the Junior Council or the Marsham Street Players at the beginning of the war (see Chapter 5), but once the bombs start falling they disappear entirely – no minutes, no annual reports of their own and no mention by anyone else. This is not altogether surprising when one considers what happened to the papers and archives of the Society in the war (detailed in the previous chapter), and at first I found archives from the 1940s impossible to locate. But while much of the spirit and experience of the Junior Council (and many of its members) undoubtedly filtered into the main Society and lived on in its DNA, there were great question marks over how it died, why it died, was anything done to try and save or revive it? More traditional-style women's organisations have great difficulty in attracting young women and have much to learn from this overwhelmingly successful attempt to do so – so much so that in the 1930s the Junior Council virtually 'steered' the whole Society.

Then in March 2015 I at last found a note in the uncatalogued minutes of the Executive Committee of the LSWS on 16 June 1943 that the Executive of the Junior Council and the main society were to be amalgamated. A later entry in 30 May 1945 confirmed that the whole of the Junior Council's Executive Committee, elected in 1938, had been merged into the main society. It was agreed that 'owing to the dispersal of the JC on war work' only a few had in practice been able to attend the meetings and that it would be desirable now to revert to the Society's rule that the Executive consist in addition to the president and the hon treasurer, of thirteen elected members. The Junior Council thus died by amalgamation, a victim of the war. One is tempted to speculate what would have happened if the war had not intervened.

Chapter 7

From small beginnings to world-class status: the growth of the Women's Library

We have already caught glimpses of the Library in chapters 5 and 6; but it is such a key part of the achievements of the Society that, even nearly forty years after it officially left Fawcett, it has to have a chapter of its own.

We have seen how the Society, by then known as the London Society For Women's Service (LSWS) had had an extremely busy and successful war but a less successful peace, at least in economic terms. They had been forced to give up their extensive premises in Victoria Street, and retreat to a small temporary home in Buckingham Gate. It was at this point – by a miraculous reversal of fortune – that a friend, Sarah Clegg, became a donor by giving the Society £1,000. This meant that they could afford to take over the former Fleece pub at 35 Marsham Street in Westminster and turn it into Women's Service House. It is at this stage in 1926 that they also felt in a position to establish a Library. They must have accumulated a tremendous amount of suffrage literature before then but this was a conscious decision to establish a collection on proper principles. An experienced Librarian, Miss Vera Douie was appointed – and was to stay in post for forty-one years – so the early Library is very much identified with her (although the Honorary Librarian Mrs Norton tended to be given more prominence). A Library Committee was also set up whose minutes are the best source of information on these early days. Just how professionally qualified Vera Douie was is not clear but she was certainly highly professional (she established the Universal Decimal System of Classification in the Library – expanding the classification of 396 for Women) – and became a name to conjure with in the library world. So it would be quite inaccurate to imply that the early Library was run in an amateurish way. Looking back sixteen years later Vera Douie reflected on the values which drove the founding of the Library:

> In founding the Library, the Committee was actuated by two motives: the preservation of the history of the women's movement in which the Society had

played so important a part, and the provision of an up-to-date collection of books and reports … useful to the newly enfranchised women now about to play their part in public life. Throughout the years a balance has been kept between these two ideas.[1]

An early photo of a small line of books on a windowsill that floats in my memory may be the first image of the library. But even the more official picture (in Ray Strachey's book *Women's Suffrage and Women's Service* published in 1927) is fairly modest. The minutes of the Library Committee, which first met on 25 January 1926, illustrate the struggle with the Finance Committee of the LSWS to get money for equipment,[2] for periodicals, for books, for Hansard and such documents (this settled in the end into an 'imprest' of £15 per quarter for books and £9 for government publications and newspapers). What the minutes also show is the very conscious effort to 'build' a library through making contact with the right government departments and other libraries, establishing a catalogue, organising an exchange of periodicals, inviting donations and indeed sending round lists of 'Suggested additions' to the Library. These last were then obviously distributed with some moral pressure, with the list annotated with notes such as 'Mrs Strachey should give', 'Only buy if Miss X can't provide etc'. Books were usually only bought if second hand, as there was never enough money and the Library was, and still is, the beneficiary of great generosity on the part of many people (Mrs Glover stands out in the early days) and very careful housekeeping. A classic example of

39. Women's Service House Library, in the late 1920s, in The Fleece at 35 Marsham Street

the latter occurred in 1928 when Bernard Shaw refused to donate *The Intelligent Women's Guide to Socialism, Capitalism, Sovietism & Fascism* and the Society sold the signature on his letter (for 15/-) to buy the book. This incident was written up in the press and condemned by the Society as inaccurate but it is there in the minutes.[3]

By the late 1920s the expanding library was beginning to outgrow the space available and some ingenious solutions were found to solve the problem, such as using the telephone box in the library for extra shelving for the Times and unbound periodicals – 'a valuable addition to the library accommodation'. But the hope of a less ad hoc solution to the space problem was in sight. Sarah Clegg, the original donor, had given a greatly increased amount to the Society and set up a Trust Fund so that they could buy the freehold of the land adjoining 35 Marsham Street and build on it. The plans included a hall and also a purpose-built library and reading room.

The Library Committee minutes of 1929 are full of plans for the move to this splendid new accommodation and its fitting out made possible by a grant from the Carnegie Trust of £485 (out of £800 in all). The result was described as 'equipment rivalling the premises in beauty and dignity'. Their plans included putting a bookrack in the window of the new premises to promote books for sale.[4]

On 2 April 1930 the Library held a party to introduce its new premises to friends and other librarians. The new setting attracted much greater activity, with more books taken out and more questions asked, and huge generosity, but it was also beginning to function as a repository for other libraries. At the end of March 1930, 330 of the books which Lady Astor had given to Crosby Hall (home of the British Federation of University Woman) arrived at the library. In 1931 the bulk of the famous largely antiquarian Cavendish-Bentinck library, donated by Ruth Cavendish-Bentinck, who subsequently took a keen and active interest in the Library, sitting on the Committee, was received. It has been kept as a discrete collection within the Library and, with additions, at the last count numbered around 2,590 volumes. The Edward Wright Library, funded by Lady Wright in memory of her son (although his father Sir Almroth Wright had been a virulent anti-suffragist) arrived at the same time. Two smaller collections – the Lina Eckenstein, on women under monasticism, and the Ada Wallas, of seventeenth- and eighteenth-century books – reached the Library in 1935. Among later additions was the Sadd-Brown collection of Commonwealth books, which was developed from 1939 in memory of the work of Diana Dollery's mother in the Commonwealth Countries League. Looking ahead, the manuscript and print archive of the Josephine Butler Society on prostitution and allied subjects built up around and after Butler's campaign against the Contagious Diseases Acts, arrived in 1956. Much time was spent integrating these additional libraries into the existing collections. All this posed problems of provenance as well as simply space – how to identify their source while merging them into the library – and various methods such as cataloguing, bookplates, coloured spots on books were adopted. People and organisations continued, and have continued, very generously to give books, archives and objects – the three strands of the Library's collection. In November 1930 the Autograph Letter Collection formed by Ray Strachey from the correspondence of Dame Millicent Fawcett was presented to the Library. It contains 'letters of absorbing interest mainly on the suffrage movement and the movement for the higher education of women, but also a hand-written letter from Queen Victoria on the death of Henry Fawcett.'[5]

We saw how hard it was to fund the Library in its earliest days. Even when it was so well housed and well appointed in the 1930s, after the move to the new site, the task of covering its running costs was not made any easier. By 1938 it had become obvious to the Executive that the Library had grown in scope and importance to such a degree that the responsibility for its support was greater than could be shouldered by a small society with about 1,400 members, mainly composed of far from wealthy professional women. So a Special General Meeting was called for 1 February and this resolution passed:

> That in view of the importance to the Women's Movement of securing the permanent establishment of a centre of authentic information on matters relating to women's work and opportunities, this SGM of members of LNSWS resolve that the objects of the Society will best be promoted by concentrating effort during the ensuing year by placing WSL upon a secure basis and desire the Executive Committee to direct their endeavours towards raising a fund for the endowment of the Library.[6]

The LSWS Junior Council, as already seen (Chapter 6, page 93), gave its support to this project, hoping that the Library, if endowed, might 'remain for all time as a record of women's work' and 'not only a permanent memorial to the women's movement, but a storehouse of fact and information'.[7] But of course this could hardly have been a less propitious time to try and raise £15,000, however charming the fund-raising brochure. 'Alas for all fond hopes' – the crises in Europe meant no money for the Library and the appeal was abandoned with less than £200 raised.

On the operational level, the Library was still a lending library but it was becoming increasingly difficult to get books returned. A notorious offender was the Duchess of Athlone, who was the first Member of Parliament to use the Library.[8] In a wonderful story Vera Douie told how the most

> curious present ever received was one given in memory of an old and faithful friend of the Society. It contained a touching inscription but closer examination revealed that the book was in fact the library's own copy which had been borrowed some time previously by a totally different borrower.[9]

The Library resolved to get tougher on 'defaulters'.

But if the Library was providing a safe haven for other collections in the 1930s, it soon found it needed a safe haven itself. Marsham Street had a terrible war, as we saw. As bombs fell, the Society's staff attempted to remain on the site, but it was felt that this was much too dangerous for the collections. Early on in the war, the main concern became to save the Library which, having escaped so far, was still exposed to continual bombing (and when priorities are identified, saving and preserving the library is always at the top of the list). German and Austrian refugees, who had seen such institutions disappear in their own countries, forced their way through locked doors to tell the librarian how signal a misfortune they would consider its closure at a time when it was so greatly needed. The Friends of the Library was set up at this time (see separate Box).

Miss Douie, who lived in Oxford, negotiated offers of accommodation from colleges there. The Library was moved to Oxford, along with a quantity of shelving, where it was established in the Society of Oxford Home Students Library (to become St Anne's), with overflows in St Hugh's College, Lady Margaret Hall and the Convent of the Sacred Heart. Despite these split sites, to everyone's relief, it did well and attracted a devoted new following. There was no acquisitions fund during the war years but Miss Douie arranged Bring and Buy sales and donated money earned through part-time munitions work. This meant she and Mrs Norton were able to search contentedly for books for the Library in the bookshops of Oxford. The only blip in this happy, if frugal, story is when Miss Douie discovered that all the rather risqué books in the Library collections had been inadvertently sent to the Convent.

Meanwhile Marsham Street, along with its beautiful library premises, was virtually derelict and was eventually – in 1947 – compulsorily purchased from the Society by Westminster Council (on which, as we saw in Chapter 5, hangs a considerable story). Part of the deal was to give the Society a preferential seven-year lease on offices in Tufton Street and to give the Library free accommodation in the Great Smith Street Public Library round the corner. So the Library came back to London, at least near if not mainly in the same building as the Society. And indeed the books were again spread around a bit, including in the office in Tufton Street, with the only purchasing budget being the proceeds of a memorial to the Society's historian Ray Strachey, who died in 1940.

40. Vera Douie, 1956

The Society still wanted a home of its own and to be reunited with the Library and started looking at freehold properties as early as 1952. In 1957 the Fawcett Society, as it had been known since 1953, with the library equally renamed the Fawcett Library, bought a new home for itself at 27 Wilfred Street in Westminster, known as Fawcett House: at last, it was thought, the Library could end its peripatetic life. This house, as we saw, inspired great affection. But accommodation for the library was not very satisfactory and archives were kept in a garden shed with consequent rodent damage, which just compounded the war damage and vandalism they had suffered in Marsham Street. Vera Douie retired in 1967 and was called to Buckingham Palace to be presented with an OBE – one of a very select band of women librarians to be so honoured. But it was very hard to pay for sufficient hours from her successor Mildred Surry; certainly by 1975 paid staffing was down to one person for two days a week, and that only thanks to a grant from the British Library. Consequently the Library became very dependent on volunteers. On the plus side a researcher, Cynthia White, was funded by the Joseph Rowntree Trust to carry out a major weeding exercise, which was becoming very necessary as more and more women's organisations were folding and placing their archives with the Library. Also one of the original aims of the Library – to help young women to participate in professions and public life – was by now being met by other libraries and organisations, so there was not the same need for the Library to hold such materials.

At first the Library did comparatively well in Wilfred Street. The Fawcett Library Trust was formed as an independent educational charity better able to qualify for tax exemptions. The Women's Service Library was transferred to the care of the new Trust and thus the new Fawcett Library was confirmed in its existence in April 1957 with the following objectives:

41. The Women's Service Library after 1929

> The advancement and promotion of education and learning by the establishment of a library dealing with the interests, activities and achievements of women at all times and in all countries, and the advancement of education and learning by these means.[10]

The Library went through a period of expansion. The Josephine Butler collections were absorbed. Money was raised for the first book to be acquired at auction, the seventeenth-century pamphlet *Advice to the Women and Maidens of London*. The archives of the Female Emigration Society and the Anglican Group for the Ordination of Women were placed with the Library. But the financial situation if anything got worse. In 1964 a new appeal was launched by Fawcett's president, Lord Bridges, with a letter in the Times.[11] The sum of £26,000 was raised between October 1964 and 1970 but much of the Fund was committed to particular projects by individuals, so the routine running costs of the Library were not eased. Its finances remained as precarious as ever. Several young researchers, including the historian Jill Liddington, remember the Library at this stage, in 1976, as a far from cheerful place:

> My abiding impression was of neglect and despondency. I felt I was trespassing into an older parallel universe, tiptoeing trepidatiously into a forgotten world on its uppers, hanging by a perilously thin thread. Were there really too few working light bulbs to cast enough light into the gloomy rooms? It seemed a 'library' at its last gasp, run by a dwindling band of increasingly frail volunteers.[12]

By 1976 it was clear that the Society could no longer sustain either the house or the growing Library, as well as the business of the Society. Westfield College, University of London, offered to take the Library but only if it could be endowed, which was clearly impossible. There were extensive and often painful discussions about the most appropriate home for the Library. The University of East Anglia was considered but felt to be too far from London. Some, including Fawcett's president Baroness Seear, argued for the London School of Economics, where it would be part of an international institution but where the books would be distributed amongst the LSE Library stock rather than kept as a discrete collection, and duplicates with their stock would not be accepted. Others argued in favour of the City of London Polytechnic, which met all the Trustees' requirements of being shelved together as a complete library in its own right and where moreover it would have Rita Pankhurst, daughter-in-law of Sylvia, as head of Library Services. In the end, after huge debate and considerable angst, the initial decision to go with the LSE was overturned and the Polytechnic (later to become London Guildhall and then in 2002 London Metropolitan University) was chosen. The Fawcett Library thus moved in 1977 as a separate entity into its own space, in the basement of the Poly's building in Old Castle Street in Aldgate. This process of decision-making galvanised and brought together older women who could just remember the fight for the suffrage with younger women from the women's movement, including a contingent from the Women's Liberation Workshop:

> …[A]fter dozens of letters and protests by members and non-members of the

Fawcett Society, a special meeting was held to make a final decision. Many women joined in order to attend and vote, and the move of the Library to the LSE was defeated in favour of the Polytechnic.[13]

This has a particular irony in view of what was to happen thirty-five years later.

The basement in Old Castle Street

The move to Calcutta House in Old Castle Street, with approximately 20,000 volumes, severed the Library's formal ties with the Fawcett Society, but Rita Pankhurst, the head of Library Services, went to great lengths to maintain links between the Society and the Library. This included working with the revitalised Friends of the Fawcett Library. They included a number of Fawcett Society activists, amongst them Mary Stott, who acted as Honorary Librarian. Mary convened a Library Liaison Committee which reported back regularly to the main Society. Rita also supported the Fawcett Annual Book Prize.

Initially Rita was only able to assign one senior full-time librarian, Catherine Ireland, to manage the Library. She was assisted by a dozen people from the Government's Job Creation Scheme allocated to help with the move. They included David Doughan, who was eventually taken on permanently as Assistant, then Research Librarian and began enthusiastically to introduce another generation of researchers (including me) to the riches of the Library. The London East End was a new experience for the Library but it flourished in its new home. Rita Pankhurst was delighted to offer it shelter and became one of its greatest champions but she was very realistic about the complexities of the move, not just physically but legally:

> The transfer of the Fawcett Library could not have taken place if the Polytechnic had not become a registered educational charity. Even so the legal complexities

42. The Fawcett Library in the basement of the City of London Polytechnic, mid-1980s

of the transfer, involving trust bodies and societies, was not resolved before 25th January, 1979, when all agreements, except one of particular technical difficulty, were duly signed. This was the result of many meetings and considerable correspondence, requiring much patience and good will on all sides, including the Charity Commissioners.[14]

Right from the outset Rita worked to raise the profile of the Library within the Polytechnic and externally across higher education, and local, national and international libraries and other cultural institutes. There was an early exhibition with the Whitechapel Art Gallery, highlighting some of the suffrage banners, posters and other visual material, and a later large exhibition by the Museum of London on suffrage. Links with the Schlesinger Library at Radcliffe College in Boston were particularly important in attracting a wide range of American researchers and a significant staff exchange. However, despite best efforts it was difficult to establish academic synergy with the City of London Polytechnic in the light of a predominantly undergraduate ethos and very restricted range of related academic activity.

Although the Library did as well as it could in the basement, after the initial year staffing levels varied, at lowest falling to about 2.5 full-time equivalent. There is no doubt it was very cramped, and this aspect was accentuated by the considerable expansion of the stock after 1977; by 2002, there were over 60,000 books and pamphlets, about 2,800 periodical titles, more than 600 boxes of archives (papers of organisations and individuals) and considerable quantities of 'museum' items such as banners, posters, photographs, campaign badges, postcards, and so on. Nevertheless, by 1987 Rita was able to record that the regular staff consisted of two full-time positions funded by the Polytechnic. A part-time assistant and cataloguer funded from a modest Fawcett Library Trust Fund worked alongside an externally funded full-time archivist and part-time photographs indexer.[15] As Polytechnic Librarian, Rita participated in fund-raising and external liaison and her administrative office also provided typing support to the library and the Friends. The Polytechnic was a generous host to the Fawcett Library but, given the external financial stringencies that affected higher education, this could lead to internal tensions.

When Rita retired in 1987 she was succeeded by her deputy Maureen Castens who continued to ensure that the Polytechnic contributions to the costs of the Library were maintained and that the new provost appointed in 1988 (Professor Roderick Floud) was made aware of the importance of the Library as a national and international research resource. She also worked with the Friends and attended the AGMs of the Fawcett Society. When the Polytechnic became London Guildhall University in 1992 Maureen was instrumental in getting the University to establish a separate Fawcett Library Trust Administering Committee with representation from the Friends to ensure that the endowment element of the Fawcett Library Trust Fund (including the £33,000 raised by the Friends) was protected and properly invested. The Committee had the additional benefit of, for the first time, providing a university-level committee with a clear focus on the Fawcett Library and a communication pathway into other university decision-making forums.[16] Maureen was further inspired by another visit to the

Schlesinger Library and by the opportunities afforded by the National Lottery Bill (which received Royal Assent in 1993). She recommended to the Fawcett Library Trust Administering Committee that the Library should appoint a new post of Fawcett Development Librarian to work up a strategic plan for the Library – this post to be funded on a tripartite basis by the University, the City Corporation and the Friends. All parties agreed to this, and Christine Wise was appointed in March 1994.

These moves turned out to be very fortuitous, given that it soon became clear that the Library's basement was very prone to flooding. A smaller flood in 1993 did not prove too disastrous but in August 1994 a major inundation, while only causing minor damage to stock, so damaged the premises that the Library had to close for many months for refurbishment. The upside to this was that the staff did not have the day-to-day work of the Library to take up their time, and could concentrate on grant applications. These were generally successful, including £225,000 over four years from the 'Non formula funding of specialised collections in the Humanities' fund of the Higher Education Council for England (HEFCE). The dried out, re-vamped basement was re-opened by the then Speaker of the House of Commons, Betty Boothroyd, on 30 June 1995, with the Provost announcing that the University intended to rehouse the Library on the site of the 1846 Wash House adjacent to Calcutta House. It was appreciated that the University would need to raise significant external sums for the building, and although Lottery funding might be a major source other funding would also be necessary for both the capital to build the building and the revenue to pay for the increased staffing that would be necessary to run it. After a false start Barbara Follett was asked to chair a Fundraising Committee with a full-time fundraiser, part-time administrative support and a number of eminent women patrons.

However these plans were affected by the major financial crisis of 1995-96 at London Guildhall which led to a major re-structuring including a 20 percent reduction of support staff and compulsory redundancies. As part of this, Library Services were brought into a new converged Academic Services with Maureen Castens as director. In the light of this it was remarkable that the University continued to maintain its commitment to rehouse the Fawcett Library and to make an application to the Heritage Lottery Memorial Fund. This was eventually submitted in early 1997. The fact that it was successful was substantially due to the continued support of the Provost and others including the Vice-Provost Deian Hopkin. The hard operational work on the Heritage application was done by Christine Wise as Development Librarian responsible for library management. A major appeal was launched with key people involved. The Business Plan stated robustly the aim: 'To create a new National Library of Women based on the internationally renowned collection of the Fawcett Library'.

The Women's Library in the Wash House
The application to the Heritage Lottery Fund was accompanied by letters of support from all sides of Parliament. The outcome in March 1998 was a grant of £4.2 million towards the new building. An appeal was made to bring the sum up to £8.3 million. The site was purchased by the University from the London Borough of Tower Hamlets, and architectural bids were invited.

*43. Façade of the
Women's Library
in the Wash
House building,
Aldgate*

The new building, which won a RIBA award, was constructed to the design of Wright and Wright Architects on the site of the old Whitechapel Wash Houses, an important amenity of social focus in the Victorian East End, which were built in 1846 and opened by Prince Albert.[17] The existing locally listed facade was retained in acknowledgement of some aspects of women's work in the nineteenth century – 'A memory of women's work'.[18] The new building rising behind the façade housed an exhibition hall, seminar room, activities room and Friends' room on the ground floor, with archive storage, reading room and staff offices on the upper floors. Artists working with the architect made beautiful pieces of art work including an installation representing significant women such as Elizabeth Garrett Anderson, Virginia Woolf and Gertrude Jekyll, which was placed in the steel grid of the staircase and lit from within by the lightwell of the stairs.

The University recognised the need to start to develop the staffing necessary to run the building and appointed a new post of Director of the Women's Library in 1999 – Antonia Byatt, who had previously run the Poetry Library and was head of Literature at the South Bank (and years before worked for the Fawcett Society). Antonia brought a fresh approach to the whole enterprise with her emphasis on exploiting the potential of the new building to open up engagement with the current debates on feminism as well as recording the past. She saw the new Library as presenting a real opportunity to bring some of the most important pieces of women's history of the nineteenth and twentieth centuries out of the basement and into the consciousness of a much wider public. The Library worked at participative partnerships which introduced new audiences to the collections: for example, a partnership with Barnardo's worked with young women who had been sexually exploited, introducing them to the Josephine Butler collections and enabling them to contribute to the exhibition. Trafficked women who were part of the Poppy project made a film about their experiences. In reflection of wider trends in the heritage world and museums to promote greater access to and engagement with their collections from the general public, the Library's programming ethos at that point was to make the collections relevant to contemporary society and to a wider audience.[19]

44. Women's Library, Aldgate, the reading room

Initial plans to re-brand the Fawcett as the National Library of Women to assist fundraising were eventually abandoned in the face of problems over trade marks, but it was felt that the designation of Fawcett Library was too limited by its connections with suffrage history, and the new name eventually chosen was the Women's Library (TWL).

This new home was opened to the public in February 2002 with a big party at which the government minister Tessa Jowell spoke alongside the Director Antonia Byatt. The Library enjoyed a correspondingly huge improvement in all its publicity materials. In the week of the opening BBC Woman's Hour broadcast contributions from a number of individuals such as Jocelyn Dimbleby, Trevor Phillips and Mary Quant about items in the collections that reflected key moments in their lives. The opening exhibition was themed around 'Cooks and campaigners'. The Library went on to flourish in its new environment, with more generous staffing levels. The number of users increased, bringing a passionate sense of devotion both to the building and to the collections; outreach to local schools and communities widened. It mounted regular exhibitions and talks: 'What women want'; 'Sinners/Scroungers/Saints: lone mothers, past and present'; 'Beauty queens, smiles, swimsuits and sabotage'; 'Art for votes' sake' (the exhibition space had been specially designed to allow the display of the Library's beautiful suffrage banner collection). It supported seminars, study days, art days, reading groups, tours and craft workshops. The figures for 2011 at the back of the Prospectus for the Women's Library show how widely it was used:

Site visits	26,820
Public programme visits	2,092
Reader visits	4,161
Space hire visits	5,064
School visits	406
Number of group visits	1,057
Reading room inquiries	14, 515
Vault retrievals	7,179

At the same time it ceased to be a lending library, started a collection of feminist zines (small-circulation, self-published magazines), worked on digitisation and the up-dating and dissemination of the cataloguing of its collections. The library received funding from the Arts and Humanities Research Council. In 2006 the collection was officially recognised as being of outstanding national and international significance by the Museums, Libraries and Archives Council (it obtained full museum accreditation in 2008); it was also recognised by HEFCE as a National Research Library for the Social Sciences.

But whatever its successes, the familiar pattern of financial insecurity was once more stalking the Library. In August 2002 a merger had taken place between London Guildhall University and the University of North London. The new institution was called London Metropolitan University, and within a short space of time its strategic and administrative centre had shifted from east to north London. The University of North London had played no role in the bid to create the new Women's Library, and doubts were now expressed about the Library's relevance to London Metropolitan's priorities. By 2011 there was familiar talk of the need for an endowment fund but in fact the situation had gone beyond this. London Metropolitan University was now going through a major financial crisis of its own and in 2012 announced that it would no longer support TWL: there was talk of opening it for one day a week for three years which, in the absence of suitable professional staff, would effectively mean the end of all library and museum functions. Bids were invited from other institutions, to be presented by the end of summer 2012. The Friends under their chair Dr Anne Summers were invited to submit criteria for the selection process, which were adopted by London Metropolitan's Selection Committee. These included the requirements to maintain the Women's Library as a distinct collection, to retain the museum artefacts together with the archives and printed collections, to offer public access on the same terms as at Aldgate, to keep up a policy of relevant new acquisitions, and to offer permanent TWL employees transfer for a minimum of two years. Bidders included Senate House (University of London), Warwick and Oxford universities, the libraries and museums of Manchester, and the London School of Economics (LSE). This last won the prize, although it offered to take only the collections, not the building. Some of those closely involved felt that LSE has the resources to look after the collections whose importance are beyond dispute.

London Metropolitan's decision aroused passionate opposition and controversy, including public demonstrations and occupation of the Library. However, no one was

forthcoming to guarantee an independent future for TWL. That the minimum running costs were now £500,000 per annum was not appreciated by protestors, not all of whom had experience of using the Library or knowledge of its recent history. However, it was hard for anyone not to see this development as a defeat, and as a betrayal of a decade of extraordinarily successful work, which had culminated in the 2011 award of 'UNESCO Memory of the World' status to some of the Women's Library collections.

The move to LSE began in spring 2013, under the supervision of Elizabeth Chapman, then Director of Library Services at LSE, and Anna Towlson, archivist and project manager. Since spring 2014 the Women's Library, known as TWL@LSE, has occupied dedicated space on the fourth floor of the LSE Library building, with the open-shelf access collections on the third floor – the latter development having required work to strengthen floorboards before this valuable facility could be restored. TWL's new Reading Room offers more than twice the seating capacity of that at Aldgate, and is also the space where LSE's other archival collections are to be consulted. Many of these – the Hall-Carpenter archive on social and sexual reform, correspondence of and relating to Helen Taylor, Octavia Hill, Beatrice Webb, Kate Courtney, Margaret MacDonald, and the Women's Industrial Council – to name only a few – 'marry' extremely fruitfully with TWL's own holdings. Two archivists and one print librarian made the transfer from Aldgate to LSE and offer not just researchers but staff – particularly in LSE's Gender Institute – the benefit of their in-depth knowledge. A ground floor space near the LSE Library entrance is dedicated to exhibitions of the archives and artefacts of both TWL and LSE Library. An exhibition on the 1866 petition and the history of the Fawcett Society will open in April 2016.

The opening of the Reading Room was marked by a grand party in March 2014 at which Mary Robinson, a former president of the Republic of Ireland, was the main

45. The Women's Library in action, 2009

speaker. The reaction from participants was extremely enthusiastic: 'What an evening. Everyone saying how great it was…I think you have created something exceptional for the Women's Library, we could not have had a better place for a home for the collections … nobody could doubt that the collection is safe with you'.[20]

The story of the Library is a remarkable one – an archetypal one of hope over experience. In all its ninety years it has never, until the last three, been anywhere near being adequately funded. It has acquired, and within ten years in the case both of the Library attached to the Millicent Fawcett Hall and the purpose-built Library attached to the old Wash House in Aldgate, lost two beautiful dedicated buildings. It has been at the point of closure. And yet in spite of these vicissitudes it has built up and managed collections on women's achievements to match any in the world. It has inspired passionate, almost visceral, devotion in those who care for it – whether as staff, Friends or researchers. Miriam David, Professor Emerita of Education at the Institute of Education writes for many:

> The women's library is an incredibly important resource of books, pamphlets and other ephemera as well as archival materials for all students and scholars or researchers of the history of the women's movement, feminism(s) and activism over the last at least 150 years. By students and scholars I mean firstly those dedicated whether in educational institutions or universities to the pursuit of feminist knowledge and wisdom to further what used to be known as 'the cause'. But of course it is much more than that one cause; it is about all the struggles and campaigns there have been not only for women's suffrage but also their economic and social liberty or liberation from women's oppression – in the family and the wider society and economic systems. Education or the pursuit of learning is fundamental to breaking down gender norms and the associated power relations that are embedded within them. So for this a library and archival resources are fundamental, even for those who are not in formal educational establishments but wish to further their knowledge and campaigning strategies to transform practices and policies.[21]

And Mary Stott, who did so much to keep the Society linked to the Library, writing in 1987, ten years after the Library had technically left Fawcett's charge, still felt: 'Of all Fawcett's activities, the Library is probably dearest to my heart, for it keeps alive the history of the "long march to equality" which has so often been forgotten or ignored'.[22]

The Library has, for most of its life, faced the challenges of poverty. It now faces the very different challenge of the need to retain its identity within a celebrated and welcoming institution which will undoubtedly take good care of it but may need to be reminded where it came from and the weight of women's hopes which it carries.[23]

THE FRIENDS OF THE WOMEN'S LIBRARY

The Friends really deserve a history of their own. There is mention of an early Friends group in the years just before the Second World War, but it was only following the Library's move to Old Castle Street in 1977 that a revitalised body of Friends emerged again. For nearly forty years they have, through their elected Executive Committee, resolutely supported the Library, in all its different homes and under all its different names. Their initial 1978 constitution was revised in 1993, 1994 and 2001 and again in 2014. Their charitable object has been 'to advance the education of the public by the promotion, support, assistance and improvement of the Fawcett Library' and its successors. Their activities are 'fundraising activities in support of the Women's Library, attracting Friends by means of Social Activities'. Their stated aims, as outlined in a paper of 3 February 2011 on the 'Proposed development of the Friends of the Women's Library', are to:

- Raise funds to improve the collections and facilities
- Promote the use of the Women's Library for research
- Encourage new readers to use the Women's Library
- Attract donations to the collections

Although the Friends have never been in a position to give large sums of money, they have been able to make their gifts very strategic and thus effective. In 1994, for instance, it was a grant from the Friends which attracted matching funding from the Corporation of London that set in motion the move towards the purchase of the Wash House for the new Library (see Chapter 7, page 104-5). Over the years they have contributed towards the conservation – or purchase – of many items in the Library such as, in 2003, Sylvia Pankhurst's drawing 'In a Pot Bank'. Between 1985 and 1990, they appealed for funds for the Library Trust Fund to provide specialist staff to look after the archival- and museum-quality items in the collections; £33,000 were raised, including £6,000 that came through Katharine Whitehorn's Radio 4 appeal in 1989. They have arranged visits and talks for their members. In the Old Castle Street years, a series of monthly meetings with speakers was held at the University Women's Club in South Audley Street. Among more recent outings was a viewing of the exhibition of Christina Broom's photographs of 'Soldiers and Suffragettes' in September 2015. And they have been able to give crucial support and advice at key moments in the Library's history, such as the move to Calcutta House in 1977. In 2012 they were invited to supply the criteria for selecting a new home for the Library, as detailed in Chapter 7, and, under their current chair Dr Anne Summers, they have been very instrumental in smoothing the Library's transition to the London School of Economics in 2013.

Chapter 8

Fawcett Society at last: the second half of the twentieth century[1]

These fifty years were marked by the Society's slow evolution into its modern form as it moved from being a volunteer-based organisation to the professionally staffed group familiar today. What did not change was Fawcett's willingness and ability to pinpoint and pursue the shifting faces of inequality as they emerged during this period, and it scored many fine achievements, sometimes on its own initiative, sometimes in co-operation with like-minded groups.

The years immediately at and after the end of the Second World War were times of difficulty and retrenchment for the Society. It had lost its beautiful, purpose-built buildings and had to retreat to a small room at 40 Broadway in Victoria; it was still separated from its Library, which did not return to London from Oxford till 1951; its renowned Junior Council had effectively disappeared and its older members, many of them from the time of the fight for the suffrage, were dying with depressing regularity – the minute books are full of sad but admiring obituaries – and new members never seemed to quite balance those who had died. It also faced a chronic financial challenge.

But in spite of these problems the Society embarked on a fair amount of what they called 'political' work. This ranged from the nationality of married women to women in the Civil Service, to social insurance (Beveridge) and taxation, the position of women in the Colonial and Foreign Offices (now both merged into the Foreign and Commonwealth Office), reform of the House of Lords and, above all, equal pay. This issue in particular dominated these years, rather as the suffrage had dominated the years before the First World War. The Society worked with the Equal Pay Campaign Committee (EPCC), supported Jill Craigie's film on equal pay (*To Be a Woman*), took part in demonstrations in Trafalgar Square, signed petitions, got questions asked in the House of Commons by supportive women MPs such as Dame Irene Ward and Dr Edith Summerskill, and made it the central plank of their campaigning work. Unfortunately this issue proved as intransigent as the fight for the suffrage had fifty years earlier and is still on Fawcett's agenda in 2016.

A great sadness was the death in June 1948 of Philippa Fawcett, seen as a 'heavy loss'.

Her contribution to the Society her mother had founded was enormous:

> The Committee look back on her life of service to the cause for which the Society stands, to the intellectual power which made her name famous and the integrity of character which inspired equal respect … Recalling her hereditary association with the Society and her particular services to it, they look back with gratitude and affection to the early years when the spare time in her busy life was devoted to work for women's suffrage and no task was too arduous nor too trivial for her to undertake and later to the period after her retirement when she brought her wisdom to the counsels of the Committee, assumed responsibility as a Trustee of Women's Service and added generous financial help to her personal work for the Society.[2]

Symbolically the laurel wreath the Society sent to her funeral was in the suffrage colours of green, white and red (see Box on suffrage colours).

The financial situation was dire. The idea to endow the Library, so that it at least would survive, came to nothing since the Library could not be treated as a charity as long as it was attached to an overtly political organisation like the Society; the gift of £6,000 given by Miss Philippa Fawcett in 1947 followed by the legacy left at her death (around £3,000) was running out; and an elaborate 'FlowerFair' organised in 1953 made a net profit of only £116.21. The Society had difficulty meeting bills and it was obvious it was running at a loss, essentially propped up by the Women's Service Trust (WST), which effectively paid the bills.

Things did look up in some respects as they entered the 1950s. For a start the Society was able, after intensive negotiation with Westminster City Council, to move into offices in the elegant 50 Tufton Street on very favourable terms, providing also the headquarters of the EPCC (under the chairmanship of Mrs Thelma Cazalet-Keir). This at last gave them room to hold meetings, receive visitors and even hire the Millicent Fawcett Hall on occasion. After the housewarming party in November 1950 two poems (if you can call them that) were copied out in the minute book, the first by Executive Committee member Miss Ahrons:

A health to the Women's Service Society
Well known for political sense and sobriety
And a health to the Lady who welcomed with pride
Has kindly consented o'er us to preside
A health to Miss Strachey, whom true to her form
We acclaim as the pilot who has weathered the storm
A health to her too who has taken her place
With her in the office we march on apace
A health to the Chairman whose clear-sighted guidance
Has helped to avoid a tragic subsidence
And a health to the members who standing together
Will uphold Women's Service though fair and foul weather

Miss Strachey very gamely responded in similar vein:

> A house may be warmed by coal, coke or peat
> Electricity, gas – even water can heat
> But the good will of friends gives the warmth that sustains
> Through Adversity's frosts with its aches and its pains
> The party that meets their glasses to drain
> And welcome prosperity's advent again
> Will be here in our midst, but others there are
> Who send good wishes and cheer from afar
> Our house will be warmed by near'uns and far'uns
> From all comes this blessing – not least from Miss Ahrons!

At an Executive Committee meeting on 3 March 1950 there was a strong call 'to restore the Society's former prosperity and vigour'. Miss Strachey became the 'Honorary' Secretary in 1951 (having been unwell much of 1948) but remained almost as fully engaged with the Society as before, although she was approaching eighty. Vera Brittain was also roped in to help. In 1951, the Library at last came back to London, to be housed in the Great Smith Street Library, also as part of the negotiations with Westminster City Council. There were problems, particularly over office accommodation for Miss Douie, but the Society was well pleased to have the Library close at hand again. Part of this new-founded confidence manifested itself in the imperative to change the name of the Society. At the annual meeting on 1 June 1951 a general consensus had formed that the present title was unsatisfactory, being too long and not descriptive of the Society's work. In February 1953 there was a competition to choose a new name. Many of the suggestions turned out to be hopelessly long-winded, such as 'The National Society for Promoting Equity and Protecting the Interests of Women', but finally the name Fawcett Society was chosen (with agreement that it should also be used as an opportunity to re-publicise the Society). It has been known as the Fawcett Society ever since.

There were some significant voices from the past. In October 1951 the Society was involved in a dinner planned by the Women's Freedom League and the Suffragette Fellowship to celebrate the golden wedding of Lord (Frederick) and Lady Emmeline Pethick-Lawrence, stalwarts of the suffrage struggle, and later Lord Frederick spoke on equal pay in the House of Lords. Fawcett also took over the arrangements for the annual commemoration service for Millicent Fawcett in Westminster Abbey, until then organised by the Association for Moral and Social Hygiene (this was a successor to groups set up by Josephine Butler in the nineteenth century and was to become the Josephine Butler Society in 1962). Less cheerfully, in 1954 Sylvia Pankhurst objected to a passage in Ray Strachey's *The Cause* and demanded it was changed.

We saw at the end of Chapter 6 how the Junior Council had fallen victim to the Second World War. Part of the JC's success had been attributed to the fact that the buildings in Marsham Street had provided the resources for it to act like a club. So when in the 1950s the Society found itself unable to cover its running costs (although of course it had the capital from the sale of Marsham Street) it initiated plans to buy a property which, apart from anything g else, could provide club facilities and hence income. The first property was investigated in 1953 and several more were considered as possibilities before 27 Wilfred Street in Victoria was finally decided upon in 1956.

The Society had no illusions about a glorious future. On 2 December 1952 it reached the conclusion that 'the Society in all probability had a limited life, although the view was expressed that there might well arise a situation when its special experience might be required to help safeguard the position of women'.

The fact was, however, that their 'special experience' was being expended in many directions – on the Women's Employment Federation, on equal rights in marriage, on employment for married women, on women in educational administration, on the Royal Commission on Civil Service pay and conditions, on the Royal Commission on taxation of projects and income, on the Equal Ministry of Women. Work on equal pay continued although sometimes not entirely straightforwardly. On 29 July 1953, for instance, the Duke of Edinburgh had referred to the topic on a visit to the Trades Union Council (TUC) but it was felt better not to draw attention to this fact! By 1955 the EPCC was organising a Milestones Dinner for 420 women to celebrate progress made, while at the same time there were calls for the Committee itself to be dissolved

Against reports that there was no money for memorials to the Garrett family in Aldeburgh, on 11 June 1954 a plaque to Millicent Fawcett was unveiled at 2 Gower Street in Bloomsbury, her home for the latter part of her life. The Society subsequently spoke to Dr D. W. Logan, the then principal of London University, to explore whether the house in Gower Street might be made available as a home for the Society but this sadly came to nothing. Negotiations, however, started for 27 Wilfred Street and in 1956 it was decided that both the House and the Library should follow the Society by taking the name Fawcett.

Political activity and financial uncertainty: a continuing story

Once installed in Fawcett House the Society had an official opening on 31 October of that year where the stewards wore the official suffrage colours of green, white and red and house-warming parties were held in the Library. A party was also given for Lady Astor, which was felt to be very moving with 'perfect' speeches and Lady Astor at her best and looking about eighteen! Parties for Vera Brittain, for the Society's president, Lord Bridges, and for the distinguished Indian diplomat and politician, Mrs V. L. Pandit, were held in 1960, but a party which Lord Bridges had planned to celebrate the ninetieth birthday of Lord Pethick-Lawrence in 1961 was overtaken by events when Lord Pethick-Lawrence died before it took place. The poetic Miss Ahrons also died and, like many members before and since, left a small legacy to the Society. Such legacies were often to prove an essential part of Fawcett's precarious finances and help to keep it afloat.

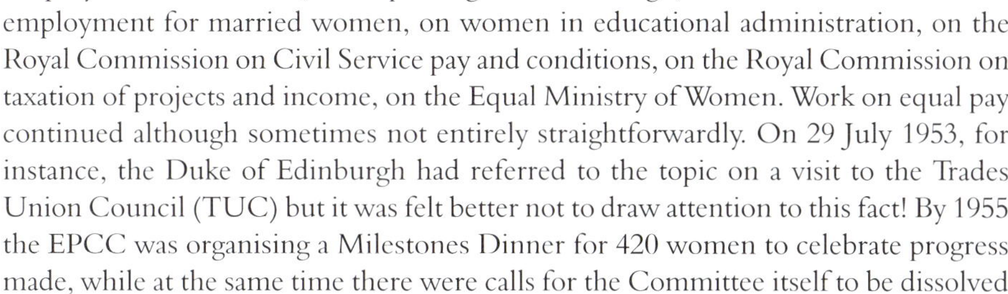

46. Blue plaque to Millicent Fawcett, 2 Gower Street, Bloomsbury

47. Philippa Strachey, in the portrait by Henry Lamb RA, 1957

Part of the general celebratory mood was the commissioning of a portrait of Philippa Strachey as she approached her ninetieth birthday. A small sub-committee was set up and fifty guineas allocated. This would, however, have only covered a drawing and it was felt an oil painting was really called for. So £250 was raised and the striking portrait still in Fawcett's possession was the result.

But beyond all the celebrations and parties was the serious political work. Fawcett listed this in its minute books under the heading of 'public questions' and an edited list of these questions during this period give an idea of the breadth of the Society's interests: women traffic wardens/ nurse training/ earnings and taxation of married women/ women mathematics teachers/ general commissioners on income tax/ National Insurance Advisory Committee/ pension schemes/women and jury service/ married women and social work/ women police pay/ education of women/ training opportunities/ women in banking/ pay of typists in the Civil Service/ married women in teaching/ age of retirement/ House of Lords reform/ TUC National Women's Advisory Committee and skilled workers/ women company directors/ women leaders in adult education/ UN Commission for the Status of Women and the UN Economic and Social Council (ECOSOC) 1960/ detention centres for girls/ discrimination by the Jockey Club against women trainers/ equal pay in the insurance industry/ the teaching profession and equal pay and, of course, the continuing battle for equal pay in general.

It looks as if there was nothing that did not come within Fawcett's sphere of interest (and this contrasts with their later much more strategic approach) but in fact they could be selective. When asked in September 1960 to support the campaign led by the National Council of Women on turnstiles in women's lavatories they declined with the words that 'this topic was outside the Society's objects and the Society could not therefore give its support'!

We have seen how Fawcett spent some time looking back to the time of the fight for the suffrage but there was also an indication of being at the dawn of a new age. In 1959 Mrs Thatcher was elected to Parliament (she became a front-bencher in 1965) and, perhaps surprisingly, was the only new woman MP to respond to Fawcett's approach, although there is not much evidence of her communicating with the Society thereafter. Mrs Castle was also mentioned for the first time and in May 1963 Betty Friedan and *The Feminine Mystique* appeared, with her argument that women cannot be expected to sacrifice the rest of their lives because of a ten-year span of childcare.

Fawcett was now adding the education of girls to its other 'public questions' and was concerned about involving young women in the forthcoming election. Amongst all its policy work – on employment, equal pay, House of Lords reform and so forth – it was finding time to complain to the BBC and other broadcasters about bias towards the suffragettes in their coverage of the fight for the vote (an argument that remains as true today). But however busy the Society was, this did not seem to help its accounts – it endlessly teetered on the edge of financial disaster with only the Trust to bail it out. It finally became clear that however careful it was with its finances, always and inevitably there was a shortfall of about £250 a year. When a decision was made that full-time secretarial help was needed, it could only be afforded because the chair, Thelma Cazalet-Keir, came up with £195 to cover the costs for the first three months. A major appeal was launched for the Library which by January 1965 had reached nearly £10,000 and it was suggested that the appeal funds might be 'borrowed from' to pay for the additional extra secretarial help.

In the area of policy concerns work continued on the issue of women in employment, and general support was given to the Josephine Butler Society with regard to their work on the Street Offences Act 1959. On equal pay it was decided that a letter should be sent to the government alongside the TUC demanding equal pay in industry. There were long lists of 'political questions' from discrimination against women trainers to judicial decisions in the field of labour law, women jurors and the British Nationality Bill. But once more the Society was not totally undiscriminating in the causes it took on, deciding, for instance, not to be involved in the Cervical Cancer Prevention Campaign on the grounds it 'was outside the aims of the Society'.

In the run-up to Fawcett's centennial year in 1966, a special meeting of the Executive Committee was held in May 1965 to clarify the committee's views on the future work of the Society, necessary before it could formulate thoughts on how to publicise it. An approach to the Women's Service Trust in the hopes of securing more income revealed there was no extra money as the WST had already taken advantage of the Trustee Investment Act 1961. In the midst of all this Fawcett House was discovered to have severe damp and the plumber produced a bill for £52.

Fawcett had been contributing to the re-working of Ray Strachey's *The Cause* (which first appeared in 1928) in the hope of a potential re-publication. But this failed to find a publisher and in the end the project was to evolve into a new book commissioned from the writer Josephine Kamm, called *Rapiers and Battleaxes: the Women's Movement and its Aftermath*, which Allen and Unwin finally brought out to celebrate Fawcett's centenary in 1966. The Society never liked the title, which it considered too aggressive. In 1965 the Society had to agree to buy a thousand copies (later reduced to 750) at cost price. It was felt that the 'responsibility on the Society for disposing of these books will be heavy but the risk was considered justified'. (This book is now on sale for 1p on Amazon, which I find rather sobering!)

In December 1965 the provisional programme for the centennial year was brought out:

7 January 1966	Fortieth birthday celebration for the Library
7 February	Commemoration of the first enfranchisement in Westminster Abbey
14 March	House of Commons lunch
16 March	Fawcett lecture at Bedford College
20 May	Centenary dinner at Fishmongers Hall
7 June	Conference and Library exhibition 26 June AGM
27 July	House of Commons lunch
October	Representative conference to review women's position and function
28 November	House of Commons lunch

The dinner was a great success, attended by 183 people, with Sir Colin Anderson and Lord Bridges presiding and Dame Kathleen Courtney in attendance – it was reported that she 'spoke well'. (Two years later, in 1968, there was some amusement when Dame Kathleen was given an editorial write-up in the women's magazine *Honey* and a champagne party introducing three new roses.) Work on equal pay and other 'public questions' (on the condition of marriage, on women doctors and on women in the diplomatic service) continued apace – but so did the acute financial problems. By September 1966 the balance in the bank was practically nil and £300 had to be borrowed from deposit. Fawcett was represented at many conferences and meetings, of the International Alliance of Women, the Commonwealth Countries League and the British Federation of Business and Professional Women.

1968 was the year in which Kathleen Halpin was re-elected chair of the Society, Mrs Castle proposed that equal pay should be introduced in industry over seven years, and Philippa Strachey, 'who for fifty years has been so closely associated with the Society', died amidst numerous plaudits from all sides of the women's movement and beyond. Fawcett decided to produce a leaflet celebrating her work with a reproduction of her portrait by Henry Lamb, to be distributed to all members with the Annual Report.

1968 was also the year when interest in equal pay was stimulated by the setting up of the UK Committee for Human Rights Year, the Suffrage Jubilee (of 1918) and Ford's women's strike. Within Fawcett a special Executive Committee meeting in November decided that the Society's resources should be put into the Library, with its own work streamlined if necessary (this was certainly not the first time that the Library has been given priority over the Society). The committee accepted changes to the Society's aims and objectives, hoped to be able to become a charity, and suggested setting up a Junior Group on the lines of the Junior Council of the 1930s. In 1969 the Society was invited to apply to join the newly formed Women's National Commission (a government advisory body) although they were subsequently considered ineligible. The Society was also turned down as a possible educational charity as its 'revised objects could not be regarded as neutral' and it was only saved from being overdrawn at the bank by a £500 grant from the WST. During this period Fawcett was campaigning on the pensions of single and divorced women (considered very discriminatory) and on matrimonial property, as well as continuing its work on equal pay.

Into the 1970s: change without and within Fawcett

The decade brought a fresh challenge for Fawcett with what was in effect, with the meeting at Ruskin College in Oxford in March 1970, the start of the Women's Liberation Movement in Britain. Fawcett were represented at Ruskin and agreed to keep themselves informed 'as observers'. By May 1971 they were hoping to arrange a meeting on Women's Liberation, with Mary Stott invited to speak 'as she is very knowledgeable and interested' in the subject. Eva Figes was also to be invited. Approaches were made to the Notting Hill Women's Liberation Workshop. The challenge of the new movement intensified Fawcett's wish to start a young people's group, although (with financial constraints firmly in mind) it would need to be one that was self-supporting. By 1972 they were planning a joint publication, *The Women's Report*, with the Women's Lobby. By 1973 this was attracting 1,000 subscriptions and brought a lot of publicity to Fawcett. But there were worries from the start that 'it had a left-wing bias' and that Fawcett would have to 'issue a disclaimer' and in December 1973 *The Women's Report* became an autonomous publication.

The 1970s were also marked by Fawcett's engagement with two major pieces of equality legislation – the Equal Pay Act of 1970 and the Sex Discrimination Act of 1975 (the SDA was intended to render unlawful certain kinds of sex discrimination on the grounds of marriage and establish a Commission – the Equal Opportunities Commission – with the function of working towards the elimination of such discrimination and promoting equality of opportunity between men and women generally). Fawcett had of course been lobbying for equal pay for decades and in 1970 expressed great satisfaction with the passing of the Equal Pay Act (although, as we shall see, that was definitely not to prove the last work they had to do on equal pay). Mention of 'the Anti Discrimination Bill' begins to appear in 1972, in February the Bill was 'talked out' in the Commons but was to be returned to the Lords. In June 1972 Fawcett's Dr Rendell was asked to give evidence to the Select Committee and in August Fawcett set up its own working party on sex discrimination legislation. By September it was commenting on the proposed legislation, contained in the government Green Paper *Equality of Opportunity for Men and Women*, including on the radio, and the Public Affairs Select Committee was responding. In February 1974 Lady Seear was emphasising the need for the Society and the women's movement in general to gear themselves up for a positive response to the proposed legislation and to work towards ensuring that the act became a living reality for women in employment. Mary Richardson was employed on a short-term contract to bring together a co-ordinating body including women's groups like the Women's Institutes and Townswomen's Guilds, religious groups, trade unions and others. The publicity campaign was led with great energy by journalists such as Mary Stott, Jill Tweedie, Shirley Conran and Claire Rayner. Mary Richardson remembers:

> We organised a range of activities to ensure the issue did not go off the agenda. My role was to help organise these activities and ensure that the Fawcett view was always influential in what was undertaken.[3]

48. Mary Stott, c. 1990

It was yet another example of Fawcett, an organisation with a numerically small membership, punching far above its weight. Many members were actively involved in the campaign and 'Baroness Seear was quite formidable and opened many doors'. By August 1974 Fawcett's sex discrimination working party was attracting some publicity to Fawcett by producing leaflets on the proposed legislation. At the same time the Society was planning a dinner to celebrate International Women's Year (1975) and supporting meetings around IWY. The dinner took place in February and raised £156. In April 1975 came the second reading of the Sex Discrimination Bill. It was passed by an overwhelming majority and in May Fawcett sent its comments on the Bill to Members of Parliament and went on to discuss the need to prepare a paper on the Bill. The SDA finally received royal assent in November 1975.

In some ways it is surprising that Fawcett had time to focus so effectively on the Sex Discrimination Bill and to take part in the heated debate around abortion legislation following David Steel's Bill in 1967 when they faced such acute internal turmoil at this period, driven by an intensifying financial crisis, the need to sell Fawcett House and to find alternative homes both for the Society and, more problematically, for the Library. By October 1976 they were suggesting that both the Society and the Library should make an inventory of all saleable items and in January 1977 they debated the future role of the Society, specifically whether it should turn itself into a 'Bureau' or continue to be a pressure group working on those areas where women are still very unequal. By March discussions centred around how, if it was to grow and expand, the Society needed central direction, a strong core, a more detailed plan and better management. This led into an examination of the future role for Fawcett's general secretary: she should select and control all staff, be responsible for all work but also be free for a certain amount of travel, visiting groups and such activities. This, however, still fell far short of the role of a director.

As Chapter 7 has detailed, intense discussions on the future of the Library continued and in October 1977 a decision was at last reached to go for the City of London Polytechnic, although dissension raged until the end. It now became urgent to sell Fawcett House and find a new home for the Society, without the Library. The house was sold for £95,000 in January 1977 and the Society got ready to move to 22/23 Albany House in Broadway in Westminster. Debates about money (of which there was never enough) centred on asking the Women's Service Trust to sell capital so there would be more money available for the Society. The investment of the money from the sale of Fawcett House meant an annual return of £6,000 to be paid out quarterly in tranches of

£1,500. There were also continuing discussions on making the Society work more efficiently, setting up a finance and general purposes committee, overhauling its rules and constitution, establishing terms of reference for sub-committees and agreeing that a close eye should be kept on Fawcett's finances. The disarray in the office had been almost total with all office procedures needing to be regulated as soon as possible by a new general secretary, yet to be appointed, whose salary scale was suggested at £3,000.

All the arrangements for moving, re-organisation and such tasks gave Fawcett little time to concentrate on other matters, although some work was done on mothers of school-age children and discussion on the founding of regional groups (although there was agreement these could not be expanded at this stage). This made the Women's Action Day organised by Mary Stott, with a steering group drawn from Fawcett and Women in Media, for 27 November 1980 even more impressive. The event was chaired by Jane Finlay, deputy chair of the Equal Opportunities Commission (EOC), and was especially memorable 'for the coming together in Central Hall Westminster of so many women's organisations of such diverse character'[4] who approved the manifesto. Many groups had information stands. The evening ended with a stirring rendering of the feminist anthem 'We are here':

> We are here, though the way is long before us,
> We are here and the world cannot ignore us,
> We will celebrate our past, and when the future's ours at last,
> Then who will dare to ask if we were there,
> Friend and mother, sister, lover,
> We were there.

Out of the Action Day came a powerful Women's Agenda, under eight headings – education, employment and training, public and political life, finance, law, family, health and media. Fifty of the women's organisations represented drafted letters to the prime minister on various points from the Agenda and delivered them to the House of Commons.

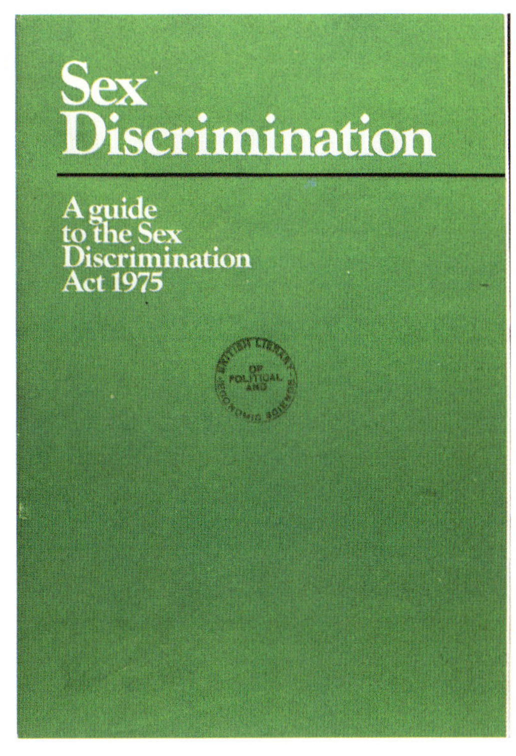

49. Sex Discrimination Act, 1975

50. *The Women's Agenda, 1980*

Fawcett initiatives

Much of the work of follow-up to the Action Day took place within Fawcett's committees – the most active being public affairs, education, employment, the media and health. The model for these fairly autonomous groups was a membership of (usually older) Fawcett members who were experts on their subjects and often met for the day in each others' homes, usually with lunch. The output of these groups was impressive. Amongst the subjects for discussion by the public affairs committee, under its indefatigable convenor Dorothy Kent, were maternity benefit, taxation of husband and wife, the Invalidity Care Allowance, violence against women, women as non-executive directors, social security, the work and constitution of the Women's National Commission (WNC), and two campaigns, the Shareholders' Question and Women into Public Life (see below). They not only discussed but lobbied relentlessly, writing to ministers and taking delegations to meet them. The health committee ran a number of important seminars, the first of which in October 1987 discussed 'the troubling issue of informed consent' and looked at women's health policy in Australia.

The education committee was particularly active with members like Valerie Evans, Jan Harding, Audrey Jones, Enid Hutchinson and Diana St John, all of whom had held senior positions in the field of education. In 1985 it resolved to draw attention to work in the UK on equal opportunities in education and training. It established the awards for positive action and published a series of influential reports. In 1989 it organised an impressive awards ceremony and conference on 'Positive Action 1989 on women's training matters: Training and vocational education for women aged 25 and over', held at the Royal Society of Arts. It was addressed by both Dorothy Wedderburn and Sandy Shulman from within Fawcett, and Carmen Cahill, director of Chatto & Windus, was the key speaker.

The memorabilia and Library sub-committee managed to find homes for the suffrage banners, with the Fawcett Library continuing to care for some. But the most important part of this committee's work was the decision to give a Fawcett Book Prize.[5] Once established, the Book Prize (awarded alternately for fiction and non-fiction, for the 'book which best contributes to an understanding of women's position in society') was to become one of the most popular and important events on Fawcett's calendar. Over the years it was to honour most of the major contributors to feminist writing.

The judges were also distinguished: in 1987, Zoë Fairbairns, Antonia Fraser and Jan Harding; in 1989, Mary Stott, Lorna Sage and Michele Roberts; in 1990, Margaret Forster, Anne Shearer and Pat Barr; and in 1991 Antonia Byatt, Shena Mackay and Janet Todd. The whole event was managed by the Library liaison committee and the prize-giving was celebrated in an elegant evening event (on one occasion, in 1986, at the Zoo), usually over dinner.

The feminist novelist Zoë Fairbairns describes the delight she felt on winning the prize in 1985:

> When Dale Spender rang me up in June 1985 to tell me that my novel *Here Today* had won the Fawcett Book Prize … I thought 'This is as good as life gets'.
>
> Why was I so pleased?
>
> Partly because it's always nice to win anything. And if the choice has been made by three of your heroes and role models – Fay Weldon, Ann Courtney and the late Mary Stott – so much the better.
>
> But there was more to it than that.[6]

Zoë went on to place the Book Prize in the context of the burgeoning feminist publishing phenomenon with at least seven self-identified feminist book publishers – Onlywoman, Virago, The Women's Press, Falling Wall, Pandora, Sheba, Stramullion – and even bookshops running feminist book weeks and sometimes fortnights. The Fawcett Book Prize made a great contribution to this, but by the mid-1990s it was felt it

FAWCETT BOOK PRIZE WINNERS

1982 Margaret Stacey and Marion Price, Women, Power and Politics (Tavistock Press)

1983 Pat Barker, Union Street (Virago Press); Zee Edgell, Beka Lamb (Heinemann Educational Books)

1984 Caroline Steedman, The Tidy House (Virago Press)

1985 Zoë Fairbairns, Here Today (Methuen)

1986 Marina Warner, Monuments and Maidens: The Allegory of the Female Form (Weidenfield and Nicholson))

1987 Shena Mackay, Redhill Rococo (Heineman)

1988 Beatrix Campbell, Iron Ladies: Why Do Women Vote Tory? (Virago Press)

1989 Stevie Davies, Boy Blue (The Women's Press)

1990 Jill Liddington, The Long Road to Greenham: Feminism & Anti-Militarism in Britain since 1820 (Virago Press)

1992 Lucy Hughes-Hallet, Cleopatra: Histories, Dreams and Distortions (Bloomsbury); Jacqueline Rose, The Haunting of Sylvia Plath (Virago Press)

1993 Jung Chan, Wild Swans (Simon and Schuster)

1994 Margaret Forster, Daphne du Maurier (Chatto and Windus)

1995 Stella Tillyard, Aristocrats: Caroline, Emily, Louisa and Sarah Lennox 1740–1832 (Chatto and Windus)

PUBLICATIONS PRODUCED BY THE EDUCATION COMMITTEE

The Class of '84: A study of girls on the first year of the Youth Training Scheme (with the National Joint Committee of Working Women's Organisations), 1985

Opening Doors to Equality of Education and Training for girls, 1986

Exams for the Boys: Report on research into sex-bias in the GCE 'O' level examination papers for 1986, ?1986

Getting Started: Positive action towards equal opportunities in vocational education and training for girls and young women 16-25, 1987

Starting Early: Equal opportunities in the primary school, 1989

Women's Training Matters: Positive action towards equal opportunities for mature women, 1989

Information Technology Matters – for Women and Girls Too! In collaboration with the Women into Information Technology Foundation, 1990

Positive Action – building on a living tradition: Fawcett Positive Action Awards, 1986–9

had had its day with much of the publicity and prestige now going to the Orange Prize for Women's Fiction established in 1996 (now known as the Baileys Women's Prize for Fiction). There was no room for two such awards and the Fawcett one was allowed to die

Fawcett was also concerning itself with women's presence in the financial and business worlds. One significant piece of work was the Shareholders Question Project out of which came the Women to the Top Campaign.[7] The origins of this go back to sometime in the 1960s when a group of like-minded women agreed, probably on an ad hoc basis, individually to attend the AGMs of public limited companies in which they held shares and to ask what came to be known as 'The Question': 'What is our company doing to appoint women/increase the number of women on the Board?'

In 1982 Dorothy Venables proposed that this scheme should be regularised and that Fawcett should target large companies, particularly those on the FTSE 100 list, with campaigners asking 'The Question' as proxies for shareholding members. However an insuperable difficulty then became apparent, in that company legislation did not allow a proxy the right to speak. At this point A. E. L. Davis initiated a parliamentary campaign, alongside general lobbying, to add the Proxies Amendment to the 1989 Companies Act. The amendment was discussed a number of times in the House of Lords, sponsored by Lady Lockwood and supported with flair by Lady Seear.[8] Despite the fact that its adoption would have benefited everybody (though principally women), the amendment was rejected in the Commons, and the provision giving a proxy the right to speak was not incorporated in Company Law until the Companies Bill of 2006 (and then without reference to Fawcett). The upshot was that, in the intervening years, the original campaign, renamed 'Women to the Top', while remaining active in theory, was disappointingly low key in practice. So when Fawcett made its structural change in the 1990s from being a voluntary-run organisation, the new management unsurprisingly did not support the shareholders campaign as a mainstream activity (coupled with which was a perceived public distaste for investment and financial matters generally as possibly elitist). Thus the outcome of this work had little effect on the overall climate of opinion regarding the problem of under-representation of women in positions of power, and a suggestion that Fawcett might be able to mount an effective campaign in the building society sector by getting one of its members into every building society to ask 'The Question' came to nothing, partly because of the lack of administrative support. The project has not, however, died completely and members of the South London Fawcett Group were attending occasional AGMs to ask 'The Question' well into the present century.

Alongside its own campaigns, Fawcett has always been ready to co-operate with other like-minded organisations in pursuit of common goals. One such collaboration, the Women into Public Life (WIPL) campaign, was a joint initiative of the Fawcett Society and the 300 Group (set up by Lesley Abdela in 1980 to try and get 300 – near parity – of women in Parliament). It was founded at a time when out of 44,000 public appointments only 15 percent were held by women. It was established in 1986, co-ordinated by Doreen Miller of the 300 Group and Margaret Joachim, chair of Fawcett, to ensure more women were appointed to public bodies, 'plugged into the networks that matter', so that appointments are not made solely on the basis of patronage. One of WIPL's tactics was to collect 500 CVs to put forward to the Public Appointments Unit (PAU) and various appointing bodies and to get leaders from all parties – David Waddington (Conservative), Jo Richardson (Labour), David Owen (Social Democratic Party) and David Steel (Liberal) – to endorse the campaign at its public launch on 21 October 1986. It went on be co-ordinated by Leah Hertz, Doreen, later Baroness, Miller and subsequently by Lily Segerman-Peck, whose part-time salary was paid jointly for three years by the 300 Group, the Fawcett Society and the EOC. The steering group consisted of the 300 Group, Fawcett, the Women's Institutes, the Townswomen's Guilds, the Women's Liberal Association, the British Federation of Business and Professional Women and the Women's Engineering Society. When Lily arrived she found hundreds of CVs waiting to be analysed and categorised, ready to be interrogated for the posts available, and shared with the PAU, with whom she established useful links. Many appointments were made as a result of this process Lily spent much of her time travelling round the country raising awareness about how women's talents can and should be used in the public sector. WIPL collected a long list of spon-

MARGARET JOACHIM'S RECOLLECTIONS

Margaret Joachim was an unusually young chair (the first of several), from 1985 to 1987, and has described to the author what Fawcett felt like from her perspective:

I chaired Fawcett during a very exciting period when many initiatives were launched or already in progress. We boosted office staff hours, and finally managed to establish the Fawcett Trust, protecting a substantial amount of our funds from taxation (including the money received when the Women's Service Trust expired). We set up Women into Public Life jointly with the 300 Group and merged our (new) media committee with Women in Media, making significant strides in improving our public profile. The Fawcett Book Prize, education awards, the Shareholder's Question Project and the campaign for non-executive directors all continued. The campaign for married women to be able to fill in their own tax returns began to show some results. A number of government departments consulted us on proposed legislation. We punched well above our weight – I often felt that if 'those in authority' had realised how small our membership actually was, they would have taken much less notice of us. But our campaigns and committees were driven forward by intelligent and capable women who had hands-on knowledge and experience of the subject matter, and they could not be easily brushed aside. Dorothy Kent retired from a senior post in the Civil Service and took up the cudgels on equal taxation and wrote letters of such authority and in such terminology that the civil servants were forced to take them seriously.

It was a transitional period – it was perhaps difficult to see at the time what progress was being made, but with hindsight we were beginning to grow in membership and starting to put the Society on a more professional footing which eventually led to today's much larger and very different organisation – but the essential principles have not changed, and unfortunately the need for Fawcett has not gone away.

soring organisations and worked closely with the WNC, which shared its concerns. But once the funding for Lily's post ran out she was only able to continue the work on an informal basis and the campaign came formally to an end, although its influence has been long lasting.[9]

In November 1987 Fawcett ran the ambitious European Colloquium for Women's Organisations together with the EEC Women's Information Service (an earlier request to do this having failed because it was not followed through by the EEC). The meeting was held in the Queen Elizabeth Conference Hall in Westminster, chaired by Margaret Joachim of Fawcett. There was debate about whether Margaret Thatcher should be asked to speak but in the end Angela Rumbold, Minister of State at the Department of Education and Science, spoke for the government. The conference was well attended

MARGARET LAIRD'S RECOLLECTIONS

In 1987, I applied for a part-time job as Joint General Secretary for the Fawcett Society … My background in trade union work, gender issues and local politics drew me to Fawcett's dingy basement in Vauxhall [46 Harleyford Road], where I found myself sharing the joint role with Antonia Byatt.[13] Fawcett was then a low-membership, highly prestigious equality organisation, developing policy and research papers aimed at influencing government ministers. It was also intent on cherishing its library of unique suffragist history and memorabilia. Our job was to service the powerful working committees who comprised the society: education, health, public affairs and so on. We also ran the annual Book Prize and events. The impression given by the (mainly) older, white middle-class members was one of cogency, rigour, hard work – a heady intellectual atmosphere, almost like a womenís college. We …employees … were treated with courtesy, but I don't remember feeling 'equal' at the beginning …

At that time, Fawcett seemed to be immutably fixed, its structure formed of the self- governing powerful committees run by long-serving, dedicated members who did huge amounts of work, often meeting in their own homes and reporting back to the Executive Committee. Apart from hoping for better premises, the prospect of development and change did not raise it head. Nonetheless, I joined Fawcett as a member as soon as I could, unable to resist the courage, determination and passion for equality that drove these formidable role models in the Fawcett basement.

Later, when I came to serve on the Fawcett Executive Committee around 1991, confidence in change, driven by a tide of great work … was already palpable under Annette Lawson as Chair. It had become self-evident to many, that for Fawcett to move forward and become a truly modern campaigning organisation, we would require to employ professionals. But no major change is easy, because it is so important to retain the expertise, experience and loyalty of the old committees, working groups and volunteers. This vital change of direction, therefore, was a test for Fawcettís famous reasoned argument approach. The final and culture-changing decision to appoint Shelagh Diplock as Fawcett's first Director, brought us firmly and successfully into the public arena.[14]

by representatives of over a hundred women's organisations and was to lead to the overwhelming approval of the resolution to set up a European Women's Lobby with the aim of providing the structure for women's organisations across Europe to meet on a regular and more formal basis. A steering committee was formed, composed of representatives of co-ordinating women's organisations from the (then) twelve member states and pan-European women's organisations. Margaret joined this group as an indi-

51. *Fawcett Book Prize poster, 1994*

vidual, with the strong moral support of Fawcett. Over the next three years, with meetings in Brussels four or five times a year, they hammered out the essentials of the principles, structure and working rules by which the Lobby would operate. They overcame the challenges of a lack of translation facilities, the fact they had no money compared with the deep coffers of the different industry lobbies, and the existence of very differing perceptions on accountability, representation, taking a political stance and such issues.

By 1990 the European Women's Lobby had received official approval, with a representative board, a paid secretariat and one or more general meetings each year, The structure has hardly changed over the years although the number of representatives has increased as the EU has acquired new members. The secretariat has also grown to accommodate an ever-growing workload and influence. And the wristwatch (with a national flag for each of the numbers) that Margaret was given as a symbolic memento of their success is still going strong twenty-five years later.[10]

At various times Fawcett has hosted the Women's Budget Group (WBG), which was founded in 1989 on the initiative of Georgina Ashworth. The Group is an independent organisation that brings together feminist economists, researchers, policy experts and activists to work towards a vision of a gender-equal society in which women's financial independence gives them greater autonomy at work, home and in civil society. WBG's view is to extend and give an institutional form to feminist scrutiny of the impact of public finance and social policy in the UK. Members contribute their expertise on a pro bono basis. It has led the way in Feminist Economics and its work complements Fawcett's campaigning approach.

Fawcett has always attracted intelligent, feminist women. When Annette Lawson (the author of an acclaimed book on *Adultery*[11]) came back from visiting professorships at Stanford and Berkeley universities in California in 1989 she found her natural home in Fawcett, rather than in universities like Brunel which in her experience displayed classic discrimination against women. She went on to be elected chair for 1990-92 and again for 1994-96 and later to play a prominent role in other parts of the women's sector, for instance in the Nat-ional Alliance of Women's Organisations and the UK NGO Commission on the Status of Women. She also chaired the international work on the Women's Nat-ional Commission, and by ministerial appointment became interim chair of the Commission. (The WNC was the UK's national machinery for engaging with and listening to the voices of women, with a direct line to government, before it was abolished in late 2010 after the election of the 2010-15 coalition government.)

It was Annette who led the move towards recruiting a more senior staff member – for the first time a director with agency, who, unlike previous general secretaries (and almost all staff in the women's voluntary sector) would actually be allowed to direct. With the appointment of Shelagh Diplock as director, Fawcett moved from an organisation run largely by its members, i.e. volunteers, to a modern professional organisation with a paid director managing a staff team, both paid and unpaid.

Many women's organisations have been unable to make this step – partly because they cannot offer the salaries and support resources needed and partly because they do not have the full backing of trustees or management committee members who like being the key people and being involved in all the tasks, rather than becoming responsible for policy but not day-to-day management. Annette found women, such as Margaret Laird (chair from 1992 to 1995), wanting to see change in both the management committee of the Fawcett Society and among the trustees of the Fawcett Trust who managed substantial funds built up by Fawcett's committed foremothers over the preceding one hundred years. These women followed careful principles of non-risk in managing the funds and gave only the necessary £11,000 p.a. or so to pay a part-time administrator and other running expenses. As a consequence Fawcett was heavily dependent on membership subscriptions and donations and on its volunteers to do the work – research, policy development and advocacy. Yet this was not viable. Its membership stayed at about 400 and there was considerable turnover. Its office was in a scruffy building in Vauxhall around which traffic streamed.[12] In one year, the basement office was burgled repeatedly. Yet in spite of this, devoted volunteers kept the work going, bringing to it their expertise in education, political representation, equal pay for work of equal value, poverty and pensions and other critical areas of women's lives and, as we have seen, often achieved great success. But to develop further this all needed translation on to another level; vision and managerial skill as well as leadership at staff level was the next step. It needed to build on its strengths to make a step change in influence and effectiveness.

Eventually the trustees of the Fawcett Trust and those of the board of the Society agreed, as did the membership, that money should be requested of the trustees to pay for a director. Within a remarkably short time, Shelagh Diplock had been chosen and turned Fawcett around, making the necessary move to decent accommodation, raising additional funding through grant-writing, bringing in new staff and running a membership drive. Over the longer term different directors have brought their own skills and vision and enabled continuing growth and the emergence of a small, credible organisation with a highly respected name to become the outstanding campaigning organisation for women's equality in the UK.

Let us not pretend, however, that nothing falls away in this professionalisation of a women's organisation. There is bound to be loss as well as gain. Some were not treated kindly and felt a sense of pain and betrayal. The necessary balance is not easy to achieve. And, as Annette said, the 'sisterhood was certainly not always very sisterly'.[15]

Shelagh Diplock was named director in 1992. Her appointment marks the end of one phase of Fawcett's existence, and so I place her perceptions in the final, contemporary chapter of Fawcett's life.

FAWCETT'S LOCAL GROUPS

Fawcett has always been keen to have local groups and indeed '[h]istorically Fawcett was a network of local activists alongside centralized campaigning and lobbying'.[1] For a time there was an active group in the northeast and in 1988 eleven regional groups were listed, although many of these were very small.[2] They could not really take off until the Local Group and Activists network was formed in 1996, funded by Barrow Cadbury, with Laura Pattinson as the regional group co-ordinator. This development was followed by briefing papers, a great deal of support in forming a group, an annual conference (in Birmingham in 1999 and Leeds in 2003) and a two-page spread 'Going local' in *Towards Equality*.[3] By March 1999 twenty-two identified groups were working on Fawcett's major national campaigns: equal pay, voting reform, under-representation, women councillors and European elections, thereby strongly boosting Fawcett's influence.

The health of the Local Groups network has depended largely on how much support Fawcett's main office can afford to give it, but in 2015, the following Fawcett groups were active: Birmingham, Bristol, Devon, East London, Leicester, Milton Keynes, North London, Norwich, Oxford, Plymouth, South London, Suffolk, Surrey/Sussex/Hants, Wakefield, West London. Three of these – Surrey/Sussex/Hants, Norwich, and Wakefield – opened in 2015. Other groups are at the end of 2015 reportedly dormant or semi-dormant: Durham, East Midlands, Edinburgh, Essex, Glasgow, Lancashire, Manchester, Merseyside, North Wales, Somerset, South Wales, West & South Yorkshire, West Sussex, and Worcester.[4]

Local groups have made a significant contribution to furthering the aims of the Fawcett Society. As examples:

- Bristol Fawcett has been very active, initially steered by Helen Mott. It has created a blog to provide up-to-date listings of women's sporting events in Bristol; in 2011 published a report on the local impact on women of the government's cuts entitled Cutting Women Out in Bristol and updated the report in 2014; and campaigned to include women on the slate and on the agenda as Bristol elected a new mayor and a new police and crime commissioner
- Fawcett Suffolk campaigned successfully in 2015 to engage women with the general election and later expanded their campaign across the whole county. Such coverage will be particularly important for the 2017 county council elections. The group recently challenged their local borough council and county council on issues relating to sexism and power, and their use of gendered language.

- Fawcett Oxford held a successful hustings during the 2015 general election

- Fawcett Devon in 2015 held a session to encourage women to join Fawcett and get involved in feminism across the southwest. The group also held a well-attended election hustings

And South London Fawcett Group (SLFG), one of the longest established, has had an impressive history.[5] It was founded in 1998. Its early meetings were held in the Bread and Roses pub in Clapham (to which I used to drive Mary Stott, who was an early member). Membership has waxed and waned but there is a small core, currently of ten or so women, who have remain loyal, dedicated and committed. Other members prefer to offer financial and/or moral support.

The Group's catchment area is large, covering the whole of South London, from Greenwich in the east to Croydon in the south and Chessington in the west. In more recent years and following the demise of other London local groups, women from central and North London have joined. To make life easier for all, most meetings take place in central London on weekday evenings.

Since 2000, SLFG has had a particular focus on lobbying the Greater London Authority (GLA) to take into account the views and wishes of South London's women. The Group conducted a postcard survey among local women to find out what they wanted from the GLA. Overwhelmingly their first priority was an improvement in public transport and, in particular, greater safety for women. The Group produced and distributed a briefing document to members of the GLA and various transport specialists and experts, including Transport for London. As a result, SLFG was invited to participate in various GLA consultation exercises and acquired a certain prestige. Lilah Edney, the Group's then chair, appeared on ITV's lunchtime news magazine, London Today.

The transport survey was followed by successive reports on women and the environment (2002), political activity (2004), pensions (2006), renewed priorities for the GLA (2009), proportional representation (2012) and the impact on local women of the budget cuts (2013). The Group has additionally run campaigns to encourage local women to use their votes in various local London and national elections. In 2009 SLFG and Fawcett North London together shone a spotlight on the lack of rape crisis funding.

SLFG has done its best to preserve links with the Millicent Fawcett Hall in Marsham Street, for so long the meeting place of the Fawcett Society's predecessors and now part of Westminster School. In 2006 and 2007 the

Group hosted events at the hall.

Fawcett's commitment to its local groups was demonstrated at their AGM on 10 October 2015, when a two-hour workshop was run by the CEO Sam Smethers and Anna Mapson, the trustee who has been 'holding' and supporting the groups until a new staff member is recruited. The importance of the groups was identified as moving Fawcett out of the Westminster village and into wider society. Strong support needs were identified, in particular better communications between Fawcett's central office and local groups, and it was emphasised that work on local groups should be part of the Society's core function and not merely a project. A Local Groups mailing a month later encouraged local groups to get involved in Equal Pay Day on 9 November, the date from which it is estimated women work for free.

Chapter 9

Equality for a new age: the Fawcett Society at 150

I have dated the 'new age' as starting for Fawcett in 1992 rather than on the millennium itself since this is the year they appointed their first director and thus moved onto a new level as an organisation. Annette Lawson, as we saw, had a strong perspective on this change. Since then Fawcett has been guided by a series of strong and able directors and chairs (another set of 'exceptional women'), often in combination, and that quality of relationship between chair and director is one of the key indicators of the strength and health of a group. (As Jane Esuantsiwa Goldsmith put it, 'the CEO/Chair position is pivotal to the success of an organisation'.) So this final chapter is substantially framed through the recollections and perceptions of Fawcett of some of these two key players, although I want first to look at a few examples of the Society's involvement with the wider world.

We saw in the last chapter how Fawcett acted as midwife at the birth of the European Women's Lobby and how Margaret Joachim went on to help it grow and develop. In 1989 Fawcett worked with the Women's Organisations Interest Group of the National Council for Voluntary Organisations (NCVO) to produce a response on the UN Convention on the Elimination of all Forms of Discrimination Against Women.[1] Fawcett was also involved in the fourth UN World Conference in Beijing in 1995. They both attended the conference in Beijing and were subsequently involved in the setting up and running of the Beijing Action Group (BAG), formed with the development organisation Change and the National Alliance of Women's Organisations (NAWO). The purpose of BAG was to ensure the implementation of the Platform for Action (the seminal document that came out of the Beijing Conference), particularly by developing relationships with government, and to allow those who had been in Beijing to continue to meet and network. BAG met for a number of years.

Shelagh Diplock, the first director, came from a campaigning background and, joining at a time when Fawcett's work was shrinking rather than growing, she was anxious to use these skills to transform the Society from an organisation which developed policy and research and wrote to ministers to one that developed strategic cutting-edge

52. 'Listen to my
vote' poster

campaigns: in other words she wanted to move Fawcett from being a think tank-style association to being an effective and high-profile campaigning group. She took up her post just before the 1992 general election and was able to use the Equal Citizenship Policy Briefings already prepared by Fawcett members for use during the election as the basis for the development of focused public campaigning activity in the years ahead.

The first two briefings were on 'Part time Workers Rights' and 'Poverty in Retirement'. To involve members and the wider public and to attract the interest of the press Fawcett developed leaflets, posters, events and lobbying materials and staged publicity stunts to attract press coverage. For instance, the Society delivered a large cake and birthday card to 10 Downing Street on John Major's sixty-fifth birthday highlighting the difference between the pensions of men and women. At that time only a third of retired women qualified for a full state pension and two-thirds were living below or just above the poverty level.

For Shelagh the appointment of a director enabled Fawcett to more fully utilise the skills of people within Fawcett, whether paid or volunteers. Members and volunteers were crucial in the development and delivery of these and later campaigns. For example, on the pensions project she was lucky enough to have the policy expertise of academics such as Dulcie Groves, Jay Ginn and Barbara Lindsay.

Fawcett also organised innovative projects to take itself and its work outside of London. In 1994 it drove a purple, decorated double-decker Eurobus – Destination 'Equality' – to visit candidates for the European Parliament, press and public in thirty-five towns and cities all over the UK during the European election campaign. The project highlighted the importance of women as voters. Managed by Jayne Ingman, this initiative met all its targets within its budget and demonstrated the benefit of having a full-time skilled specialist on the staff. It was also the start of an important and influential strand of Fawcett's work, drawing the attention of politicians and the press to the key role of women's votes in elections. The 'Listen to my vote' campaign developed by Fawcett's first campaigns officer, Mary-Ann Stephenson, in the run-up to the 1997 general election brought the Fawcett Society to the attention of a new generation of politicians and, in contrast to just five years earlier, women began to feature in press coverage and in the campaign literature of all parties.

Fawcett also began working with larger better-funded organisations outside the usual women's sphere. One example was the 1996 Low Pay campaign, where Fawcett worked closely with the Royal College of Nursing and the Low Pay Unit. Fawcett developed two posters: 'What do you get if you pay peanuts' featuring a nurse; and 'Men wouldn't wear it' with two blokey men dressed as charladies, which were distributed by the RCN and trade unions to a multitude of workplaces.

This new vision of a modern campaigning organisation allowed Shelagh to bring in new grant money, and Fawcett's income rose significantly to £267,000 in 1998 (although it was always easier to raise money for projects than for core costs – still true of the voluntary sector as a whole). The financial contribution of the membership, which by the time Shelagh left in 1998 had grown to around 2,500, was nearly £50,000 per annum. The increase in membership and higher profile around the country also helped Fawcett gain a grant from the Barrow Cadbury Trust to support the develop-

MEN WOULDN'T WEAR IT.
You wouldn't catch most men accepting the low money and status that 'women's jobs'
like cleaning, caring and catering attract.
CONTACT US AND HELP TO RAISE THE VALUE OF WOMEN'S WORK.
EQUAL PAY · EQUAL VALUE · EQUAL PARTNERS
fawcett
The Fawcett Society, 5th Floor, 45 Beech St, London, EC2Y 8AD. Tel: 0171 628 4441.

ment of a local groups network. A full-time project worker, Laura Pattinson was appointed and by 1998 there was a network of developing groups around the country (see Box on local groups).

New people were becoming active in Fawcett. Shelagh was lucky to have the support of first Annette Lawson and then Margaret Laird as Fawcett chairs – and Sandy Shulman as chair of the Fawcett Trust. But she also made a positive effort to attract and involve energetic young feminists like Karen Sayer, Jenny Watson and Karen Ross, originally as volunteers and later on to the committee. The improved financial position enabled Fawcett to rise out of its basement to new premises in Beech Street in the Barbican, thereby providing a much better working environment for both staff and volunteers.

In the second half of 1997 Fawcett's brilliant exhibition, 'Funny Girls: Cartooning for Equality', developed by curator Diane Atkinson,[2] opened in Manchester and subsequently in London. The exhibition attracted much attention and high-profile support, even if the failure to find a sponsor and the too high costs of the project led to a significant funding gap of £90,000 (the Fawcett Trust stepped in to help with funding to limit the deficit to £5,000). Mary Stott celebrated her ninetieth birthday at a reception at the exhibition.

The exhibition helped to cement relationships with many well-placed people including key figures within the new Labour government. Fawcett now spoke of itself proudly as a feminist organisation with T-shirts proclaiming 'This is what a feminist looks like'. The directors and chairs who followed built on these advances. Each brought her own special skills to enable Fawcett to extend its influence.[3]

Jenny Watson came in as chair when Shelagh was director. She had been impressed by 'wonderful' Fawcett women such as Dorothy Wedderburn, Sandy Shulman, Margaret Joachim and Margaret Laird, who backed her all the way. She went on to develop a strong relationship with Mary-Ann Stephenson when the latter became director in 1998. After the 1997 general election many more women in Parliament became interested in Fawcett's work. Fawcett was careful to work with women from all parties. They had a lot to say about candidate selection, about Scotland and Wales, about childcare, about women's income and the Women's Budget Group, about the interest from the media in women's issues and about the cohort of women journalists like Lucy Ward at the *Guardian* and Gaby Hinsliff.

When Jenny left to become deputy chair of the Equal Opportunities Commission in 2001, she felt she was leaving Fawcett in a better state than she could have imagined given the difficulties, including financial difficulties (women's organisations had been very bad at asking for money but she was quite unembarrassed about doing so!). She felt there was still a need to focus on women in political life. But she also saw the urgency for pushing for both women and men to get the working and family lives they want. As well as continuing to focus on how women's lives are still different from men's, she argued in an email to the author, 'Fawcett will need to continue to find a way to show how stereotyping women also limits the choices for men. It will have too to be thoughtful about the differences amongst women because some of us have far more choices about our lives and our careers than others'.[4] Jenny is delighted Fawcett is still

54. Fawcett's 'Funny Girls' cartoon exhibition, 1997, poster

here but feels there are still things it has not yet challenged and issues it has still not addressed.

Jenny's words might be seen as an attempt to express a concern that many have – that equality is not just about breaking glass ceilings and earning large salaries but also about articulating a different set of values based on care.

When Mary-Ann Stephenson was named director in 1998, she took over a very young and diverse staff (although this did not apply to the membership). The Women's Budget Group (WBG) – made up of academics and both Fawcett and TUC members – was getting going, as noted in Chapter 8. After the 1997 election the government, partly through Anna Coote, developed much stronger links with the voluntary sector, and there was a feeling of doors opening. The WBG wrote a response on tax credits, arguing they should go to the main carer, usually a woman and the government changed its policy in response. Fawcett had much more access to government advisors. Katherine Rake was working in the government's Women's Unit, and there was great deal of expertise to draw on amongst academics.

Fawcett set up its Commission on Women and the Criminal Justice System – covering victims, offenders and those who were working in the system – as a result of concern about the differential impact of current laws and practices on women in England and Wales. In the 2001 election Vera Baird, who had been on Fawcett's executive, was elected to Parliament and established parliamentary links with the Society. She became chair of the Commission, which held its first hearing (on victims and witnesses) in February 2003 and its last, a visit to Holloway prison, in January 2004. Its findings were published not just in the final report in March 2004 but in a number of interim reports (which are listed among Fawcett publications in Appendix 3). The successful execution of this Commission brought Fawcett considerable acclaim.

The 2001 election greatly raised Fawcett's media profile. 'The Listen to my vote' campaign, backed up by the research into women's voting patterns by academics like Joni Lovenduski and Pippa Norris, got the idea across that women's political priorities mattered. Media coverage, once secured, escalated. Fawcett was on the Today programme and in the national press (but didn't break into breakfast television). Stronger political representation, stalls and meetings at all party conferences, including a meeting addressed by Cherie Blair at the Labour conference in 2000, increased exposure. Fawcett developed relationships with Labour MPs and with sympathetic Tory women like Teresa May and Caroline Spelman. They linked with the Bow Group around women's representation. Among local groups, Bristol was doing work on violence against women from a feminist perspective. (In retrospect Mary-Ann felt local groups should have concentrated on local issues.)

These years were also marked by an ongoing struggle with the expert groups about who spoke on behalf of Fawcett, who should write letters direct to ministers. As part of its trend towards a more professional style of organisation and management, the Fawcett office tried to draw up terms of reference, advising that everything had to be 'signed off' before it could be sent. The expert groups were unable to agree to the new terms of reference. Their ways of working were not compatible with those being introduced by Geethika Jayatilaka, the head of policy and public affairs, their experience, though extensive, was not the only kind required, and they were judged to be both unaccountable and elitist. There was a need for clarity of vision, not just the ability to write letters. The problem seemed to be an intergenerational one. In the end, the groups were disbanded. This inevitably caused distress to those who had given their time so generously. Inevitably 'modernisation' has brought loss as well as gain. But in retrospect Mary-Ann felt she could have handled the process of change management better, been more sensitive to the work the groups had done. Fawcett has still not really been able to find a better mechanism to draw on the enormous expertise which it has among its members and this remains a challenge.

When Mary-Ann first came in as campaign manager there were two-and-a-half staff; when she left there were six. She felt she was leaving Fawcett in a good state but still with no firm funding base (it is think tanks that get corporate funding rather than campaigning groups). When she left, Fawcett was seen as credible. She could get meetings with politicians, media coverage and funding. Her view is that Fawcett needs an executive board that can ask difficult questions. It is obviously a liberal feminist organisation but has the advantage of being both 'insider' and 'outsider' simultaneously.

Jane Esuantsiwa Goldsmith became chair in 2001, the first black woman to take the role. She saw this fact as significant since, in her words, 'diversity and black and minority ethnic women become one of our big strategic priorities in terms of policy development, action and recruitment'. Fawcett already had a diverse staff but not at the most senior level or on the board. As she pointed out, her election 'enabled Fawcett to reach out to more people and to become a role model for other black women who aspired to leadership roles'.

Jane had worked as a management consultant and brought other specific and very

55. Mary Stott and Katharine Whitehorn at Mary's ninetieth birthday party

56. Bill Bailey in Fawcett's 'This is what a feminist looks like' T-shirt

useful skills to Fawcett from her experiences in the key fields of women's budget, equal pay, international development and anti-poverty, as well as with black and minority ethnic women. Her additional experience as a strategist with many voluntary sector organisations allowed her to run participatory strategy development processes with wide participation. She was able to make Fawcett not only more diverse but more member orientated and created a more integrated feminist organisation, one well structured and supportive, based on feminist principles of leadership and management that would empower everyone in the organisation and lead to constructive feedback, accountability and reporting.

At the beginning of this century, the perception of Fawcett was of a middle-aged, middle-class, white, fairly traditional woman's group with a very good track record in lobbying and legislative change. What Jane was trying to work towards was a Fawcett in the future that would be a key player in an alliance bringing together Feminist Economics, the women's movement and women politicians to become thought leaders in an alternative vision of women's rights and quality of life. Such a vision should be inclusive, internationalist, working with sister organisations across the globe and speaking to all diverse members of society: a whole women's movement that would take a much more integrated and strategic approach, developing a joint feminist vision of an alternative society in which the care economy and quality of life is central to policy and practice.

Katherine Rake was director of Fawcett from 2002 to 2009. She came from the government's Women's Unit and before that was an academic at the LSE. She thus brought strategic and academic rigour and had already written for Fawcett before she joined as director. She worked with four chairs – Jane Esuantsiwa Goldsmith, Sue Tibballs, Michelle Mitchell and Angela Mason (the director of Stonewall who served from 2007 to 2013). She feels Fawcett has been on a long journey of professionalisation, updating its constitution, becoming a charity and becoming incorporated. These processes have given the organisation weight.

Katherine gave Fawcett's work a strong economic force with work on pensions (with Age UK), on caring duties and on the gender pay gap. She worked on the Criminal Justice project with Vera Baird and also worked to get more black women into Parliament. Among her strengths was a skill in raising trust income. In her time Fawcett's income trebled and she was able to move the office to Berry Street in Clerkenwell.

In conversation, Katherine said she saw Fawcett's past, particularly its emphasis on women's rights (and the suffrage colours Give (Green) Women (White) Rights (Red)) as very significant. This early identification of the suffragist element of the women's movement gave Fawcett the gift of understanding the broad and interconnected reasons for women's equality. Her view is that this history needs to continue to inspire, rather than narrowly define, the organisation. She felt she left the organisation much stronger, with an agenda which incorporated concerns about cultural sexism and where she observed considerable new energy, particularly among younger feminists. According to Katherine, Fawcett was and is in a position to tie things together across women's life course (e.g. work on the older women's agenda) and across social, economic and cultural aspects of sexism. The cross-party support Fawcett cultivated during this time was also considerable, and its clout and reputation among parliamentarians was a great advantage as it helped shape and influence policies. There have been some issues with radical feminists, she pointed out, e.g. over sex workers, but on the whole communication has been good and these issues did not have an impact on the daily working of Fawcett. She thought subsequently Fawcett had been wrong to go for the Judicial Review in 2010. The Society, nonetheless, is absolutely still needed; there may have been progress but there has also been a backlash, with old issues showing themselves in new manifestations, as with the issue of teenage girls with low self-esteem, who are miserable about their body image.[5]

Sue Tibballs was chair from 2003 to 2005. Among her recollections of her time in office, she remembers the 'big challenge' of trying to expand the membership. She 'oversaw a wholesale review of Fawcett's brand and positioning aimed at making the organisation's role and ambition more accessible and engaging.' This involved overseeing 'the whole process from writing briefs to appointing an agency'. The brand was carried over to all applications from web to newsletter and to the magazine's *StopGap* title. Sue feels it has served Fawcett well and still looks 'fresh and relevant' today. A more

rights-based brand introduced in recent years has been replaced once more by the brand Sue introduced. She was also involved in the Inspiring Women events at Cadogan Hall, ahead of their time.

These testimonies reveal a strong organisation with, as the publications list in Appendix 3 makes clear, a bedrock of substantial, authoritative research reports – on poverty, criminal justice, representation, black and minority ethnic women, money, benefits, the gender equality duty, the Gender Equality Forum, race and gender, boardroom quotas, gender stereotyping, corporate sexism, equal pay[6] and sex and power. These have ensured that all campaigns run by Fawcett have been underpinned by considerable intellectual rigour and have received extensive and (mainly) serious coverage in the press.

Fawcett has also been a courageous organisation – never more so than in August 2010 when under the brave leadership of Ceri Goddard as director and Angela Mason as chair it took the unprecedented move of applying for a judicial review of the government's 2010 'emergency' budget. Fawcett tasked the courts to examine whether the budget had been drawn up in accordance with the law – in particular the government's legal duty under the Equality Act (2006/2010) to give 'due regard' to the impact that different measures have on men and women. Fawcett's argument (supported by the Women's Budget Group) was that some £5.8 billion of the £8 billion of cuts contained in the budget were to be paid for by women through cuts in housing and maternity benefits and the public sector pay freeze. Fawcett appointed the solicitor Samantha Mangwana, of Russell, Jones and Waller solicitors and the QC Karon Monaghan, both of whom worked pro bono.

In the event the judicial review was not allowed but the government was clearly quite shaken by the challenge and it certainly did not endear Fawcett to Mrs Theresa May.

The Society has sought to replicate some of the glamour of the Book Prize dinners and events going right back to the Millicent Fawcett Hall with evenings like Inspiring Women. Although Fawcett does not exist for social reasons it has always been good at giving a party!

Despite its achievements, Fawcett has had several setbacks since the beginning of the

57. Getting Fawcett's message out

twenty-first century. One director never got beyond the probationary period, and an interregnum before Sam Smethers was appointed CEO in 2015 meant that for many months the organisation had effectively to be run by its chair Belinda Phipps. In 2014 it was subjected to bad publicity in the tabloid press over the provenance of its 'This is what a feminist looks like' T-shirt, had to cope with a deficit and has had three different addresses since it left Berry Street in 2013.

But its AGM on 10 October 2015 was very upbeat. It revealed an organisation that for the first time in five years had a modest surplus. It did not play down the challenges. As the chair reported:

> It has been a dynamic year for the charity in which we've moved offices, developed our IT infrastructures, established new funding sources, recruited a new CEO and a new Head of Policy and Insight. There was a high level of necessary staff turnover.

The need was to 'enable Fawcett to set the right organizational culture to prepare for and deliver on the 150th anniversary and beyond'.[7] The report covered three main strands of policy work on 'Women and poverty', which included 'Closing the income gap', and 'Women and power' with the general election campaign and hustings and the successful #ViewsnotShoes campaign, which monitored the media coverage of women MPs. 'Sustainable Fawcett' was the third strand, to build Fawcett's capacity to deliver its policy objectives in its 150th year with such essentials as the website, the database, membership engagement and the online shop.

Belinda Phipps, having held Fawcett together during a difficult period, is particularly concerned about sustaining Fawcett as an organisation:

> What the history of the Fawcett Society shows very clearly is that Fawcett has always punched well above its weight but hasn't consistently looked after itself very well, leaving it vulnerable at times. Together with the board I am determined to change that so that we can strengthen the organisation for the future, grow our impact and change society for the better for women and men. The overwhelming message is that feminism needs a strong Fawcett Society.[8]

58. Staff, volunteers and members at Fawcett's AGM 2015

Jenni Murray, Fawcett's president, speaking at the open panel after the AGM, looked to the future with confidence:

> As President of Fawcett for more than ten years I've seen the society go through some difficult times. Fund raising is no picnic for any charity and membership fell during what was known, erroneously, as the 'post feminist' era. But, in true suffragist fashion, Fawcett has continued its research and lobbying work to achieve equality between men and women and has never been afraid of shouting loudly in a strong feminist voice. Support is now rising among younger generations. Much has been achieved in the past 150 years, but Fawcett has never been more relevant.[9]

Fawcett has gained all its successes within a wider sector – the women's voluntary sector – in which it has been notoriously difficult to operate. Women's rights have never been a popular cause (even the minister for women has almost invariably been given other responsibilities) and even when achieved have frequently been subsequently eroded. Women's organisations are unsurprisingly chronically underfunded, which makes the struggle more difficult. At the same time women's organisations have faced problems of governance and leadership, often believing that women cannot misuse power in the same way as men and that being 'sisters together' will somehow of itself ensure peace and harmony.[10] Unsurprisingly they have been, often painfully, disabused of these beliefs and have had to strive to build structures which enable and protect both individuals and groups. For Fawcett this has meant years of struggle not only fighting for women's rights but also to create the sort of vehicle or organisation which makes the struggle possible

There are many, many ways one could measure Fawcett's success and influence and we have mentioned some of them. Just three tiny but significant contemporary – or near contemporary – indicators: the work of the Fawcett Society, and in particular the role played by Millicent Fawcett, were marked in October 2008 by a special Royal Mail issue of six stamps featuring 'Women of distinction', which spanned the whole of the twentieth century. Millicent featured on the first class stamp with the caption 'Suffragist VOTES FOR WOMEN. Millicent Garrett Fawcett'. Then on 12 September 2015 at the last night of the Proms (the very heart of the establishment), conductor Marin Alsop gave an impassioned plea for gender equality, and in December 2015 a small display on Millicent Garrett Fawcett went up for a nine-month period at the National Portrait Gallery. There, in one of the small ironies of history, in her display case, Millicent comes perhaps for the first time face-to-face with one of her old adversaries, a large portrait of Lord Balfour. As I was repeatedly told: if Fawcett did not exist it would have to be invented. Its relevance in 2015-2016 is well illustrated in the debate over Jeremy Corbyn's all-male senior Labour team.

All in all Fawcett's achievements are remarkable. While honouring its famous past it has refused to let that past define it but has built on it to become the effective campaigning organisation it is today and the active and pioneering force it aims to be in the future. This should be both a comfort and a safeguard to us all. Certainly the new director, Sam Smethers, seems to be more than up for the challenge:

It is a privilege to be leading the Fawcett Society as it approaches its 150th year and to have the opportunity to stand on the shoulders of the great women who have gone before me. Reflecting on their experiences and their contributions, it is clear that despite its many challenges Fawcett has been a defining and constant force in the fight for women's rights and gender equality. It is also exciting that feminism is seeing a resurgence, giving renewed energy and impetus to the cause. Fawcett has never been more relevant.[11.]

Notes

Introduction

1   Ray Strachey, *Millicent Garrett Fawcett*, London: John Murray, 1931, p. 6.
2   Ray Strachey, *Women's Suffrage and Women's Service: The History of the London and National Society for Women's Service*, London: London and National Society for Women's Service, 1927, p. 5. I am much indebted to this book particularly for the period in the early part of the twentieth century.
3   Elizabeth Crawford, *Enterprising Women: The Garretts and their Circle*, London: Francis Boutle Publishers, 2002, p. 241. I am likewise extremely indebted to this book, which I have consulted constantly.
4   Sheila Herstein, 'The Langham Place circle and feminist periodicals of the 1860s', *Victorian Periodicals Review*, 26/1 (Spring 1993), p. 24.
5   Crawford, *Enterprising Women*, p. 240.
6   Strachey, *Millicent Garrett Fawcett*, p. 19.
7   Quoted in Crawford, *Enterprising Women*, p. 242.
8   The painting's full title is, decidedly unsnappily, *An Incident in Connection with the Presentation of the First Women's Suffrage Petition to Parliament in 1866*. It is in the possession of The Women's Library@LSE.
9   Strachey, *Millicent Garrett Fawcett*, p. 42.
10 Ibid.
11 Ibid., p. 44.

Chapter 1 Disappointment and defiance

1   Ray Strachey, *The Cause: A Short History of the Women's Movement in Great Britain*, preface by Barbara Strachey, London: Virago, 1978, p.109 [reprint of first edition, published London: G. Bell and Sons Ltd., 1928].
2   Strachey, *The Cause*, p. 110.
3   See *The Punch Book of Women' Rights* by Constance Rover, London: Hutchinson, 1967. See also Brian Harrison, *Separate Spheres: The Opposition to Women's Suffrage in Britain*, London: Croom Helm, 1978, for a compelling account of the strength of the opposition.
4   Strachey, *The Cause*, pp. 112-13.
5   Under this act all women living within certain areas, e.g. military and naval centres, were liable, on police accusation, to be declared 'common prostitutes' and as such compelled to undergo periodical intimate medical examination. There was no such requirement for men. Josephine Butler worked tirelessly for the abolition of this law, achieving its repeal in 1883.
6   Preface by Shelagh Diplock to Diane Atkinson's *Funny Girl: Cartooning for Equality*, London: Penguin, 1997, p. xvii.
7   See Constance Rover, *Women's Suffrage and Party Politics in Britain 1866-1914*, London: Routledge & Kegan Paul, 1967, p. 2.
8   Rover, *Women's Suffrage and Party Politics*, pp. 2-3.
9   'The Queen is most anxious to enlist every one who can speak or write to join in checking this mad, wicked folly of "Women's Rights" with all its attendant horrors, on which her poor feeble sex is bent, forgetting every sense of womanly feeling and propriety.' See Sir Theodore Martin, *Queen Victoria as I Knew Her*, Edinburgh; London: William Blackwood, 1908, p. 69, quoted in Rover, p. 34.
10 See Rover, *Women's Suffrage and Party Politics*, pp. 4-5.
11 I was particularly interested to discover – from Ann Dingsdale's extensive research – the significant part which my home area of Blackheath played in the beginnings of this campaign. J. S. Mill was living in Blackheath Park when he presented the petition, Elizabeth Garrett and Emily Davies both had Blackheath connections – and seventeen brave local women signed the petition. See Ann Dingsdale, '"Generous and lofty sympathies": The Kensington Society, the 1866 women's suffrage petition and the development of mid-Victorian feminism', Ph.D. thesis, University of Greenwich, 1995, online at: http://gala.gre.ac.uk/6380/1/Dingsdale_1995_DX195214_COMPLETED.pdf.

12 Rover, *Women's Suffrage and Party Politics*, p. 23.

13 Strachey, *The Cause*, p. 276.

14 Strachey, *The Cause*, pp. 122-23.

15 See Elizabeth Crawford, *The Women's Suffrage Movement: A Reference Guide 1866-1928*, London: Routledge, 2001, for further details on these suffrage campaigners.

16 Speech by Mrs Fawcett at the Annual Meeting of the Central Committee of the National Society for Women's Suffrage, 15 July 1890, from LSE Library's collections, 2LSW/A/2/2, Box OS07.

17 Strachey, *The Cause*, p. 265.

18 *Female Suffrage: A Letter from the Rt. Hon W .E. Gladstone MP to Samuel Smith MP*, 11 April 1892, published as a pamphlet by John Murray, London, 1892. Quoted in Rover, *Women's Suffrage and Party Politics*, p. 120.

The fight for education

1 They entered the popular imagination with verses such as: Miss Buss and Miss Beale/ Cupid's Dart do not feel,/ They leave that to us,/ Poor Beale and poor Buss. Quoted in Jane Robinson, *Bluestockings: The Remarkable Story of the First Women to Fight for an Education*, London: Penguin, 2010, p.36.

2 Strachey, *The Cause: A Short History of the Women's Movement in Great Britain*, London: Virago, 1978, p. 127.

3 The list of universities of the British Isles with the dates of their foundation up to 1940 is to be found at http://www-history.mcs.st-andrews.ac.uk/history/Davis/index.html under 'Statistics for each University'. I am grateful to A. E. L. Davis for information on this website.

4   London: Nick Hern Books, 2013.

5 Henry Maudsley, 'Sex in mind and education', *Fortnightly Review*, 15 (January-June 1874), pp.467, 472, quoted in Robinson, *Bluestockings*, p.71.

6 Strachey, *The Cause*, p.260.

7 There is a brief biography of Philippa Fawcett at http://www.lms.ac.uk/library/special-collections. My thanks again to A. E. L. Davis for drawing my attention to this website.

Chapter 2 Into militancy

1 *Rover, Women's Suffrage and Party Politics*, p. 122.

2 See Jill Liddington and Jill Norris, *One Hand Tied behind Us: The Rise of the Women's Suffrage Movement*, London: Virago, 1979, for an excellent account of this rare working-class group of suffragists. 'Yet for thirty years, they had been in the vanguard of working women in Britain. The radical suffragists had been their mouthpiece; from a position of unique industrial strength they had fought for a whole range of feminist demands which would affect women in all aspects of their lives', p. 276.

3 Liddington and Norris, *One Hand Tied Behind Us*, p. 23.

4 Andrew Rosen, *Rise Up, Women!: The Militant Campaign of the Women's Social and Political Union, 1903-1914*, London: Routledge & Kegan Paul, 1974, p. 29. I am much indebted to this book for details of the history of the WSPU.

5 Rosen, *Rise Up, Women!* p. 49; he refers to the *Manchester Guardian*, 16 October 1905, and the *Sunday Times*, 8 March 1908.

6 Rosen, *Rise Up, Women!* p. 53.

7 Leslie Parker Hume, *The National Union of Women's Suffrage Societies, 1897-1914*, New York: Garland Publishing, Inc, 1982, p.32. I am likewise much indebted to Leslie Parker Hume for her detailed account of the development and work of the NUWSS.

8 Rosen, *Rise Up, Women!* p. 57.

9 For an idiosyncratic view of this period, including very lively sketches, see Yoshio Markino's *My idealed John Bullesses*, London: Constable and Co. Ltd., 1912. Although he concentrates mainly on the suffragettes, he shows massive admiration for Mrs Fawcett, whose book *Political Economy for Beginners* he had read as a boy.

10 Rosen, *Rise Up, Women!* pp. 107-08.

11 Ibid., p. 116.

12 From LSE Library's collections, 7HFD/D/33, Elsie Duval's prison diary record of being forcibly fed.

13 Rosen, p. 128. Gladstone papers, British Museum. Add.MSS 46067, H. Gladstone to E. Hobhouse, London, 9 November 1909. [These papers are now held at the British Library.]

14 Hume, *The National Union of Women's Suffrage Societies*, p. 50.

15 Ibid., p. 59.

16 Letter from H. N. Brailsford to M. G. Fawcett, dated 18 January 1910. Manchester Libraries, Information and Archives, reference GB127.M50/2/1/291. Reproduced by courtesy of Manchester Libraries, Information and Archives, Manchester City Council.

17 Jill Liddington, *Vanishing the Vote: Suffrage, Citizenship and the Battle for the Census*, Manchester: Manchester University

Press, 2014, p.201. This gives an excellent account of the whole anti-census campaign.

18 From LSE Library's collections, 7MGF/A/1/053 and 054. Lloyd George's letter is reproduced by kind permission of the Parliamentary Archives and the Lloyd George family.

19 Hume, *The National Union of Women's Suffrage Societies*, p. 123.

20 In 2013-14, Tate Britain in London mounted an exhibition of Sylvia's work which most prominently displayed her series on 'Women at work', produced in the north in 1907.

21 Speech by Mrs Pankhurst at the Pavilion Theatre, 10 February 1913, TNA, HO 45/10695/231366.

22 Hume, *The National Union of Women's Suffrage Societies*, p. 134, quoting the *Manchester Guardian*, 24 February 1912.

23 Hume, *The National Union of Women's Suffrage Societies*, p. 153. Millicent Fawcett justified this change in NUWSS tactics in an article, 'The election policy of the National Union', that appeared in *The Englishwoman*, 14/42 (June 1912), pp. 241-45.

24 Hume, *The National Union of Women's Suffrage Societies*, p. 198.

25 Strachey, *Women's Suffrage and Women's Service*, pp. 21-22. The banners mentioned in this extract form an important part of the museum collection of The Women's Library@LSE.

26 Hume, *The National Union of Women's Suffrage Societies*, pp. 72-73.

27 See Kate Parry Frye's *Campaigning for the Vote: Kate Parry Frye's Suffrage Diary*, edited by Elizabeth Crawford, London: Francis Boutle Publishers, 2013.

Suffrage Colours

1 See Lisa Tickner, *The Spectacle of Women: Imagery of the Suffrage Campaign 1907-14*, London: Chatto & Windus, 1987, appendix 6 on Suffrage Colours, p.265. See also Diane Atkinson, *Suffragettes: The Purple White & Green: London 1906-1914*, London: Museum of London, 1992.

2 *The Common Cause*, 25 November 1909, p, 433.

3 Letter from Anne Walton to the Director, Shelagh Diplock, 6 February 1998.

Chapter 3 Loyal citizens

1 Quoted in Rosen, *Rise Up, Women!*, p. 248.

2 Katherine Connelly, *Sylvia Pankhurst: Suffragette, Socialist and Scourge of Empire*, London: Pluto Press, 2013, p. 68.

3 See Sylvia Pankhurst, The *Home Front: A Mirror to Life in England During the First World War*, London: Hutchinson and Co., 1932, chapter 19.

4 *Towards Permanent Peace. A Record of the Women's International Congress held at The Hague, April 28th-May 1st, 1915*, London: British Committee of the Women's International Congress, June 1915, p. 14. I am deeply indebted here and elsewhere in this chapter to Helen Kay's research on the Women's International League of Peace and Freedom and its origins in 1915.

5 *Towards Permanent Peace 1915*, p. 4; and Pankhurst, *The Home Front*, p. 153.

6 *Jus Suffragi*, 8/13 (September 1914), p. 1.

7 *Jus Suffragi*, 8/13 (September 1914), p. 160.

8 Quoted in J. Vellacott, 'Feminist consciousness and the First World War', in *Women and Peace: Theoretical Historical and Practical Perspectives*, edited by Ruth Roach Pierson, London and New York: Croom Helm, 1987, pp. 114-36.

9 Felicity Ruby and Edith Ballantyne, 'Beyond armistice: women searching for an enduring peace', *Open Democracy* 50.50 series, 1 September 2014. Online: https://www.opendemocracy.net/5050/felicity-ruby-edith- ballantyne/beyond-armistice-women-searching-for-enduring-peace.

10 Strachey, *Millicent Garrett Fawcett*, p. 277.

11 Strachey, *Women's Suffrage and Women's Service*, pp. 25 and 28.

12 Ibid., p. 26.

13 Ibid., p. 29.

Chapter 4 From suffrage to service

1 Strachey, *Women's Suffrage and Women's Service*, p. 30.

2 Ibid., p. 31.

3 Strachey, *The Cause*, p. 373.

4 Ibid., p. 375.

5 Extracts from Millicent Garrett Fawcett, 'Women Voters', *Times* [London, England] 6 June 1924, page 10. *The Times Digital Archive*. Web. 4 March 2015. See also Millicent Fawcett's handwritten draft of this letter, 3 June 1924, from LSE Library's collections, 7MGF/A/1/234, Box 2.

6 Strachey, *The Cause*, p. 384.

7   Stanley Baldwin's letter is reproduced with the kind permission of Earl Baldwin of Bewdley.

8   Strachey, *Millicent Garrett Fawcett*, p. 349.

9   'Dame Millicent Garrett Fawcett Memorial', *Times* [London,England] 12 March 1932, page 15. *The Times Digital Archive*. Web. 4 March 2015.

10 'Dame Millicent Fawcett', *Times* [London, England] 14 March 1932, page 11. *The Times Digital Archive*. Web. 4 March 2015.

11 One of the 'unintended consequences' of this refurbishment was that in May 2013 members of the South London Fawcett Group were invited to visit the Abbey workshops and see the renovation work in progress.

Chapter 5 Rooms of their own

1   See entry in Minutes book for 18 October 1881. From LSE Library's collections, 2LSW/A/4/1/1, Box FL135.

2   Strachey, *Women's Suffrage and Women's Service*, p. 34. I went looking for these early buildings. Number 9 Berners Street has become the Berners Hotel, but most of old Victoria Street did not survive the Second World War and redevelopment. I was intrigued to find the site of numbers 56 and 58 has rather appropriately become the Department for Constitutional Affairs, whose strapline is 'Justice, Rights and Democracy'. I feel we should perhaps tell them this and suggest a plaque to an earlier struggle for just these things!

3   *Strachey, Women's Suffrage and Women's Service*, p. 35.

4   Marion Crofton was also the great-aunt of my friend Jo Rogers and it was through the happy occurrence of researcher's serendipity that I came across her wonderful scrapbooks.

5   Minutes book of the LNSWS Executive Committee, 16 April 1929. From LSE Library's collections, 2LSW/A/4/1/1/12, Box 139.

6   Hermione Lee, *Virginia Woolf*, London: Chatto & Windus, 1996, p. 598.

7   *The Diaries of Virgina Woolf*, edited by Anne Olivier Bell and Andrew McNellie, London: Hogarth Press, 1977-1984, vol. 4, pp. 6-7.

8   'Professions for Women', in Virginia Woolf, *A Room of One's Own* and *Three Guineas*, edited by Michèle Barrett, London: Penguin, 1993, p. 360.

9   The accounts of the buildings during the war years are drawn from Executive Committee minutes for that period. These may be consulted in LSE Library's collections, 2LSW/A/4/1/1/19-21, Boxes FL 141-142.

10 See Executive Committee minutes, 21 May 1941.

11 Ibid.

12 Executive Committee minutes, 27 November 1940.

13 Executive Committee minutes, 12 May 1943 (which recorded the resolutions to be put at the AGM).

14 Executive Committee minutes, 22 March 1944.

15 Damage to E Block of Romney House in Tufton Street was recorded officially when a V1 bomb exploded on 2 July 1944 in a hit on the building. See City of Westminster Archives Centre, C. D. 131.10, nos 1858-1904, incident 1882.

16 Executive Committee minutes, 8 October 1944. Minutes are understandably sparse at this point but it is astonishing how calmly these traumatic events are recorded.

17 Executive Committee minutes, 8 November 1944.

18 Executive Committee minutes, 8 July 1949.

19 Dr Cynthia White's papers await cataloguing, so the poem cannot yet be referenced.

20 Paper on 'The future of the Fawcett Library', dated 31 October 1976, signed by the Library trustees J. Coulson, K. Halpin, S. Rothwell and W. J. Smith. From LSE Library's collections, 7PMA/03/03, folder 2.

21 Undated paper on the Women's Service Trust accompanying the Fawcett Society's Annual Report 1976-1977. See LSE Library's collections, 2LSW, Records of the Fawcett Society and its predecessors, folder on 'Women's Service Trust. Exc Summary of History 1926-1977'.

22 Letter to the Chair, 15 January 1985.

23 The part played by Project W and other organisations and actors is recorded in LSE Library's collections, 7ENH/Survey 9/2, Box 9, and 2LSW/X/Survey 3/20.07, Box 20.

24 Letter from Marquess of Anglesey to Councillor David Weekes, leader of Westminster City Council, 18 February 1992.

25 Letter from Save Britain's Heritage, 28 April 1992.

26 Letter from Department of National Heritage to Dr Lynne Walker, 21 May 1992.

27 This situation is not unique to women's organisations. Shelagh Diplock, Fawcett's director in the early 1990s, describes having lunch with three powerful women who all ran beautiful, historic and listed buildings – Chatham House, the international think tank, was one. All felt it was a great responsibility which detracted from their main purpose.

The Women's Service Trust and charitable status

1   This and subsequent quotations come from a paper by Kathleen Halpin on 'Women's Service Trust' in the Fawcett Annual Report 1976-77. I am deeply indebted to Sandy Shulman for giving me access to her archive on Fawcett's trusts as well as advising on the text

2   Personal communication, 10 September 2015.

Chapter 6 'You have won rooms of your own'

1   See first Annual Report of the Junior Council, 1927. From LSE Library's collections, 2LSW/J/12, Box FL 248.

2   Junior Council Annual Report 1935, pp.6-7.

3   These reports, which run from 1927 to 1939, may be consulted at The Women's Library@LSE, where they are catalogued under 2LSW/J/12, Box FL 248. Each report runs from 1 April of one year to 31 March of the next.

4   See Junior Council Annual Report 1929, p.8.

5   Ibid., p.8.

6   Quoted in Ray Strachey's *Millicent Garrett Fawcett*, pp.350-51.

7   Minutes of the Executive Committee of the Junior Council, 24 October 1929. From LSE Library's collections, 2LSW/J/12, Box FL 248.

8   Proceedings of Junior Council Annual Meeting, 24 April 1931, p.4 of Junior Council Annual Report 1931.

9   Junior Council Annual Report 1931, p.7.

10   Proceedings of Junior Council Annual Meeting, 27 April 1932, p.7 of Junior Council Annual Report 1932.

11   Junior Council Annual Report 1932, p.15.

12   Junior Council Annual Report 1933, p.12.

13   Junior Council Annual Report 1934, p.8.

14   Ibid., p.9.

15   Ibid., p.13.

16   Junior Council Annual Report 1935, p.7.

17   Ibid., pp.13-14

18   Junior Council Annual Report 1936, p.5.

19   Ibid., p.9.

20   Ibid., p.13.

21   Proceedings of Junior Council Annual Meeting, 29 April 1937, p.8 of Junior Council Annual Report 1937.

22   Proceedings, p.10 of Annual Report 1937.

23   Junior Council Annual Report 1937, p.3.

24   Ibid., p.3.

25   Ibid., p. 4.

26   Ibid., p.7.

27   Junior Council Annual Report 1938, p. 2.

28   Ibid., p.4.

29   Junior Council Annual Report 1939, p. 2.

Chapter 7 From small beginnings to world-class status

1   Vera Douie, *Women's Service Library: The First Sixteen Years 1926-1942*, London: London and National Society for Women's Service, 1942 [unpublished typescript], p. 2.

2   In 1926 the need was greatest for shelving, filing cabinets, chair, a lamp, etc. See Library Committee minutes for 22 April, 21 July, 3 November 1926 (LSE Library's Collections, 2LSW/L/1/01, Box 388). Rugs came later in 1927, two presented by Mrs Glover, and in 1928 a stepladder to reach high bookshelves.

3   Library Committee minutes, 19 September 1928. The minutes for the years 1928-1930 may be read at LSE Library's Collections 2LSW/L/1/02-04, Box 388.

4   Library Committee minutes, 9 January 1929.

5   Library Committee minutes, 3 November 1930.

6   Vera Douie, *Women's Service Library*, p. 6.

7   Junior Council Annual Report 1938, p. 2. From LSE Library's collections, 2LSW/J/12, Box FL 248.

8   Library Committee minutes, 6 February 1930.

9   Vera Douie, *Women's Service Library*, p. 7.

10   Annual Report of the Society and Library 1957, p. 14. See LSE Library's collections, TWL@LSE Special Collections pamphlets, 305.4206041 FAW.

11   Letter from Lord Bridges, *The Times*, 28 October 1964. *Times* [London, England] 28 October 1964, page 11d. *The Times Digital Archive*. Web. 4 March 2015.

12   Jill Liddington, 'Fawcett saga: remembering the Women's Library across four decades', Archives and Sources, *History*

Workshop Journal, 76 (October 2013), pp. 266-80.

13 From article on 'Fawcett Library' in *Women's Report: A Bimonthly Feminist News Magazine*, 5/1 (November-December 1976).

14 Rita Pankhurst, 'The Fawcett Library: the acquisition of a special collection', *COPOL Newsletter* (July 1979), p. 23.

15 See Rita Pankhurst, 'Collection development and women's heritage: the case of the Fawcett Library', in *Women's Studies International Forum*, 10/3 (1987) [special issue on 'The Fawcett Library: Britain's Major Research Resource on Women Past and Present'], pp. 225-39.

16 For example, Maureen's position paper calling for a better baseline of quantitative information about the collections led to the University Research Committee granting funding for an extensive Resource Survey of the Collections carried out by the Archivist, Anna Greening.

17 See website of London Borough of Tower Hamlets, www.towerhamlets.gov.uk/lgsl/601-650/623_walks/east_end_life_featured_walks/the_heart_of_the_old_east_end, accessed 19 September 2015.

18 Clare Wright, partner in Wright & Wright Architects, in *Building Design*, Issue 1509 (9 November 2001).

19 Personal communication with Antonia Byatt.

20 From the commemorative booklet produced by The Women's Library@LSE, 12 March 2014.

21 Personal communication.

22 Mary Stott, 'At the heart of the matter', in *Women's Studies International Forum*, 10/3 (1987) [special issue on 'The Fawcett Library: Britain's Major Research Resource on Women Past and Present'], pp. 221-23, p. 221.

23 I am immensely indebted to David Doughan, Maureen Castens and Anne Summers – all key players at different times in the Library's history – for their considerable and invaluable contributions to the second half of this chapter.

Chapter 8 Fawcett Society at last

1   I am indebted to the staff of the Women's Library at LSE for identifying material for this chapter from LSE Library's collections, 2LSW/A/4/1/1/21-22 and 2LSW Minutes of the Executive Committee, July 1959-December 1964; January 1965-April 1968; May 1968-September 1976.

2   Committee minutes, 27 October 1948.

3   Personal communication, September 2015.

4   The Fawcett Society Annual Report 1980-81, Report of the Executive, year ending 1 May 1981, p. 5.

5   Ibid., p. 6.

6   These reflections come from an unpublished paper written by Zoë Fairbairns for a Fawcett meeting on 'Story telling: Why Women's Fiction deserves a prize' on 16 April 2014. In the event family illness prevented her giving it in person.

7   I am grateful to A. E. L. Davis for her valuable input to this paragraph.

8   See Hansard Parliamentary debates, House of Lords official report a) Vol. 505 No. 61, 6 April 1989, cols. 1283–1290, b) Vol. 506 No.76, 27 April 1989, Cols. 1380–1384. On 6 April Baroness Lockwood moved amendment No. C15, arguing that despite there being many women in public life of proven ability, of the top 200 holding companies, only about 2 percent had women directors. In support, Baroness Seear pointed out that the intention of the amendment was not to secure a quota: what was asked for was 'a positive policy' of investigating 'whether there are not women of the qualities required – perhaps at a higher degree than the available men who might be appointed.' On 27 April Baroness Lockwood confirmed what Baroness Seear had said.

9   See LSE Library's collections, 8WAT/C/C.

10   I am indebted to personal communications with Margaret Joachim for information on the origins and formation of the European Women's Lobby and on her time as chair.

11   Annette Lawson, *Adultery: An Analysis of Love and Betrayal*, paperback edition, Oxford: OUP, 1990.

12   This was 46 Harleyford Road where it moved in 1982.

13   Antonia has her own recollections of this period: she felt as if the Society had important things to say but didn't have the capacity to make itself heard. It was run by a committee, which included 'extraordinary' members like Mary Stott and Jenni Murray (who used to breastfeed her baby in the basement in Harleyford Road), and the paid roles focused on servicing the membership rather than campaigning (personal communication).

14   I am grateful to Margaret Laird for this insight into Fawcett's process of change (personal communication, 29 October 2015).

15   I am indebted to Annette Lawson for her insight into this transitional stage of Fawcett's development (personal communications, 31 August 2015 and 10 October 2015).

Fawcett's local groups

1   See Jo Littler and Helen Mott, 'Going local', in the Fawcett Society's magazine of those years, *Towards Equality*, Summer 2003.

2   Regional Membership Report 1988, written by Margaret Laird; author's own archive.

3   Jo Littler and Helen Mott, 'Going local', in *Towards Equality*, Summer 2003.

4　Email from Anna Mapson, 21 September 2015.

5　Many thanks to Janet Scott, secretary of SLFG, for preparing this account. Lest I be accused of special pleading I should declare an interest in that I am a long-term, if latterly not very active, member of SLFG.

Chapter 9 Equality for a new age

1　See *Eliminating Discrimination: A Long Way to Go: A response to the UK Government's initial report on the UN Convention on the Elimination of all Forms of Discrimination Against Women (CEDAW)*, Fawcett and the Women's Organisations Interest Group at NCVO, March 1989.

2　See Diane Atkinson, *Funny Girls: Cartooning for Equality*, London: Penguin Books, 1997.

3　I am very grateful to Shelagh Diplock for her considerable contribution both here and at different parts of the narrative.

4　And I am very grateful to Jenny Watson for her input here.

5　My thanks to Katherine Rake for her input here.

6　Equal pay has been a perennial issue for Fawcett from the 1960s (see Chapter 8) – and indeed even going back to the 1930s – and the chair, Belinda Phipps, was still writing to the *Times* under the heading 'Closing the pay gap between men and women' (15 July 2015) about the implementation of Section 78 of the 2010 Equality Act which requires companies with more than 250 employees to publish details of what their employees are paid.

7　The Fawcett Society, Report and Financial Statements, year ended 31 March 2015, p.3.

8　Personal communication with Belinda Phipps.

9　Personal communication with Jenni Murray.

10　Jane W. Grant, *The Governance of Women's Organisations: Towards Better Practice*, CIS Commentary No. 104, Centre for Institutional Studies, University of East London, May 2002.

11　Personal communication with Sam Smethers.

Bibliography

Atkinson, Diane. *Suffragettes: The Purple White & Green: London 1906-1914*. London: Museum of London, 1992

Atkinson, Diane. *Funny Girls: Cartooning for Equality*. Preface by Shelagh Diplock. London: Penguin, 1997

Banyard, Kat. *The Equality Illusion: the Truth about Women and Men Today*. London: Faber and Faber Ltd., 2010

Connelly, Katherine. *Sylvia Pankhurst: Suffragette, Socialist and Scourge of Empire*. London: Pluto Press, 2013

Crawford, Elizabeth. *The Women's Suffrage Movement: A Reference Guide 1866-1928*. London: Routledge, 1991

Crawford, Elizabeth. *Enterprising Women: The Garretts and their Circle*. London: Francis Boutle Publishers, 2002

Dingsdale, Ann. "'Generous and lofty sympathies": The Kensington Society, the 1866 women's suffrage petition and the development of mid-Victorian feminism'. Ph.D. thesis, University of Greenwich, 1995

Douie, Vera. *Women's Service Library: The First Sixteen Years 1926-1942*. London: London and National Society for Women's Service, 1942 [unpublished typescript]

Fairbairns, Zoë. *Here Today*. London: Methuen, 1985

Fairbairns, Zoë. 'Story telling: Why Women's Fiction deserves a prize' Unpublished paper written for a Fawcett meeting, April 2014

Fawcett, Millicent. *Women's Suffrage: A Short History of a Great Movement*. London: T.C. and E.C. Jack, 1912

Fawcett, Millicent. 'The election policy of the National Union'. *The Englishwoman*, 14/42 (June 1912), pp. 241-45

Fawcett, Millicent. *The Women's Victory – and After: Personal Reminiscences, 1911-1918*. London: Sidgwick and Jackson, 1920

Fawcett, Millicent. *What I Remember*. London: T. Fisher Unwin, 1924

Fawcett Society, and the Women's Organisations Interest Group at NCVO. *Eliminating Discrimination: A Long Way to Go: A response to the UK Government's initial report on the UN*

Convention on the Elimination of all Forms of Discrimination Against Women (CEDAW), March 1989

Female Suffrage: A Letter from the Rt. Hon W .E. Gladstone MP to Samuel Smith MP, 11 April 1892. London: John Murray, 1892

Frye, Kate Parry. *Campaigning for the Vote: Kate Parry Frye's Suffrage Diary*. Edited by Elizabeth Crawford. London: Francis Boutle Publishers, 2013

Grant, Jane W. *The Governance of Women's Organisations: Towards Better Practice*. CIS Commentary No. 104. Centre of Institutional Studies at University of East London, May 2002

Harrison, Brian. *Separate Spheres: The Opposition to Women's Suffrage in Britain*. London: Croom Helm, 1978

Herstein, Sheila. 'The Langham Place circle and feminist periodicals of the 1860s'. *Victorian Periodicals Review*, 26/1 (Spring 1993), pp. 24-27

Hirsch, Pam. *Barbara Leigh Smith Bodichon 1827-1891: Feminist, Artist and Rebel*. London: Chatto & Windus, 1998

Hume, Lesley Parker. *The National Union of Women's Suffrage Societies, 1897-1914*. New York: Garland Publishing, Inc, 1982

Kamm, Josephine. *Rapiers & Battleaxes: The Women's Movement and its Aftermath*. London: George Allen and Unwin, 1966

Lawson, Annette. *Adultery: An Analysis of Love and Betrayal*. Oxford: OUP, 1990

Liddington, Jill. 'Fawcett saga: remembering the Women's Library across four decades', Archives and Sources, *History Workshop Journal*, 76 (October 2013), pp. 266-80

Liddington, Jill. *Vanishing the Vote: Suffrage, Citizenship and the Battle for the Census*. Manchester: Manchester University Press, 2014

Liddington, Jill, and Jill Norris. *One Hand Tied Behind Us: The Rise of the Women's Suffrage Movement*. London: Virago, 1979

Markino, Yoshio. *My idealed John Bullesses*. London: Constable and Co. Ltd., 1912

Pankhurst, Rita. 'The Fawcett Library: the acquisition of a special collection'. *COPOL Newsletter* (July 1979), p. 23

Pankhurst, Rita. 'Collection development and women's heritage: the case of the Fawcett Library'. *Women's Studies International Forum*, 10/3 (1987) [special issue on 'The Fawcett Library: Britain's Major Research Resource on Women Past and Present'], pp. 225-39

Pankhurst, Sylvia E. *The Home Front: A Mirror to Life in England during the First World War* London: Hutchinson and Co., 1932

Pankhurst, Sylvia E. *The Suffragette Movement*. London: Longmans, Green and Co Ltd. 1932

Pierson, Ruth Roach (ed). *Women and Peace: Theoretical Historical and Practical Perspectives*. London and New York: Croom Helm, 1987

Rosen, Andrew. *Rise Up, Women!: The Militant Campaign of the Women's Social and Political Union, 1903-1914*. London: Routledge & Kegan Paul, 1974

Rover, Constance. *The Punch Book of Women's Rights*. London: Hutchinson, 1967

Rover, Constance. *Women's Suffrage and Party Politics in Britain 1866-1914*. London: Routledge & Kegan Paul, 1967

Ruby, Felicity, and Edith Ballantyne. 'Beyond armistice: women searching for an enduring peace'. *Open Democracy* 50.50 series, 1 September 2014

Shulman, Sandy. 'We walk in the footsteps of some exceptional women'. Annual Report of the Fawcett Society, 1987-88

Stott, Mary. 'At the heart of the matter'. *Women's Studies International Forum*, 10/3 (1987) [special issue on 'The Fawcett Library: Britain's Major Research Resource on Women Past and Present'], pp. 221-23

Strachey, Ray. *Women's Suffrage and Women's Service: The History of the London and National Society for Women's Service*, London: London and National Society for Women's Service, 1927

Strachey, Ray. *The Cause: A Short History of the Women's Movement in Great Britain*. London: G. Bell and Sons Ltd., 1928. [Reprinted, with preface by Barbara Strachey. London: Virago, 1978]

Strachey, Ray. *Millicent Garrett Fawcett*. London: John Murray, 1931

Tickner, Lisa. *The Spectacle of Women: Imagery of the Suffrage Campaign 1907-1911*. London: Chatto & Windus, 1987

Towards Permanent Peace. A Record of the Women's International Congress held at The Hague, April 28th-May 1st, 1915. London: British Committee of the Women's International Congress, June 1915

Vellacott, J. 'Feminist consciousness and the First World War', in *Women and Peace: Theoretical Historical and Practical Perspectives*. Edited by Ruth Roach Pierson. London and New York: Croom Helm, 1987, pp. 114-36

Vernon, Betty D. *Congratulations, Dr. Stott*. London: Betty D. Vernon, 1997

Women's Report: A Bimonthly Feminist News Magazine. 'Fawcett Library'. 5/1 (November-December 1976)

Wright, Clare. 'A memory of women's work'. *Building Design*, Issue 1509, 9 November 2001

Appendix One

Principal gatherings organised by the Junior Council, 1926-39

Junior Council parties, talks and meetings

1926-27

'Engineering as a profession for women', speaker Caroline Haslett, Secretary, Women's Engineering Society (20 January 1927)
Two talks on professions for women at the Bar and in solicitor's work, speakers Miss V. Stephenson and Miss I. Stoney (17 February 1927)

1927-28

'Journalism', speaker Norah Heald, editor of *The Queen* (31 May 1927)
'Opportunities in departmental stores', speaker G. E. Todd (28 June 1927)
'Women in the Civil Service', speaker Miss Sanday (28 June 1927)
'Women in trade unions', speaker Mrs Blainey (28 September 1927)
'The work of a literary agent', speaker Audrey Heath (28 October 1927)
'Should married women work?', speakers Dora Russell and Lady Trustram Eve (24 November 1927)
'Matrilineal civilisation', speaker Mrs Aitken (23 January 1928)
'Juvenile delinquency', speaker Miss Clement Brown (23 February 1928)

1928-29

'The future of women in public life and in industry', speaker Arthur Greenwood MP (17 May 1928)
'American labour legislation as affecting women and children', speaker Beryl Power, deputy chief inspector, Trades Boards, Ministry of Labour (25 October 1928)
'Openings in science for women today', speaker Major A. G. Church, secretary of Association of Scientific Workers, followed by four women speakers (4 December 1928)
'Politics as a career, a pleasure and a duty', speaker Mrs Oliver Strachey, Viscountess Astor present (31 January 1929)
Parties on forthcoming general election, 11 January, 4 March, 26 April 1929

1929-30
'The animals at the Zoo', speaker Mr Seth-Smith, Zoological Society (13 June 1929)
At Home for Katherine Mayo, author of *Mother India* (10 July 1929)
'The romance of insurance', speaker Edith Beesley (24 October 1929)
Talks by Lilian Barker, governor of HM Borstal Institution for Girls, and Mary Stopford on probation (25 November 1929)
'The film industry', speaker Miss J. M. Harvey, Secretary to the Film Society (26 February 1930)
At Home for the Secretaries to the Delegates to the Naval Disarmament Conference (4 March 1930)
Joint meeting with the LNSWS on LNSWS and the Royal Commission on the Civil Service (19 March 1930)

1930-31

'The degree of co-operation at present possible between men and women in the same occupations', joint meeting with the LNSWS (2 April 1930)
'The Old Vic', speaker Lilian Baylis (23 May 1930)
'The development of civil aviation and women's part in it', speaker Sir Samuel Hoare (8 July 1930)
'The serious uses of broadcasting' and 'The work of the Central Council', speakers Mr Stobart, Miss Mary Somerville (12 November 1930)
'Music and literature', speakers Dame Ethel Smyth, Virginia Woolf (21 January 1931)
'Women's prospects in commerce today', four speakers (16 February 1931)
'The various aspects of the publication of books', four speakers (13 March 1931)

1931-32

'What my party offers to the woman voter', speakers Jennie Lee, Irene Ward, Aline MacKinnon (20 May 1931)
'The present day problem of housing', three speakers, chaired by Elizabeth Scott (8 July 1931)
'The Indian frontier and the Hindu Koosh', speaker Brigadier-General Hon. Charles Bruce, CB (15 October 1931)
'The history of French art', lecture by Miss C. Prescott (21 January 1932)
'Some aspects of the book world', speaker Basil Blackwell (29 January 1932)
'Later history of French art', second lecture by C. Prescott (18 February 1932)
'An editor at bay', speaker Tom Clarke, editor of the *News Chronicle* (22 February 1932)

1932-33

At Home for women MPs (29 April 1932)
'What the forthcoming World Conferences can do for recovery', speaker Sir Alfred

Salter (7 July 1932)
'Men, women and work in Russia', speakers Hubert Griffith, H. W. Smith, David Low, cartoonist (18 October 1932)
'The Ottawa Conference', speaker Malcolm Macdonald MP (18 January 1933)

1933-34

'The history of original engraving in England', speaker Campbell Dodgson (8 November 1933)
'The administration of a modern teaching hospital: where the money comes from and where it goes', speaker H. L. Eason, Superintendent, Guy's Hospital (12 December 1933)
'The economics of prosperity' (on the social credits system) (28 February 1934)
'Dictatorships in Central Europe', speaker G. P. Gooch (19 March 1934)

1934-35

'Fascism is incompatible with free speech', debate between Professor Harold Laski and Major Yeats-Brown (19 April 1934)
'Pacifism and national defence', speaker Sir Norman Angell (2 October 1934)
'Britain – the pharisee?', speaker Geoffrey Crowther of the *Economist* (November 1934)
'Equal pay – ought we to have it and how can we get it?', speaker Miss E. A. Ford, Board of Education and chair of the Council of Women Civil Servants (4 December 1934)
'European police: the Saar Force and its significance', speaker Horsfall Carter (17 January 1935)
'Proposals for constitutional changes in India', speaker Lord Lothian, joint meeting with the LNSWS, (7 February 1935)

1935-36

'The trial of Sir Thomas More', speaker Richard O'Sullivan KC (15 May 1935)
'Behind the screens', speaker Andrew Buchanan (5 June 1935)
'That women won't be freed', sherry party, speaker Miss Arnot Robertson (22 October 1935)
'Discoveries in Egypt and Palestine', speaker Miss M. A. Murray (20 November 1935)
'Chinese art', speaker Constance Prescott (16 January 1936)
'How the Swedish women reached their present-day position', speaker Baroness Palmstierna (3 February 1936)

1936-37

'Children's reading down the ages', speaker Elizabeth Sprigge, chaired by Noel Streatfeild (2 April 1936)
'The open-air theatre' (in Regents Park), speaker Sydney Carroll (23 June 1936)

 'Lewis Carroll and "nonsense"', speaker Walter de la Mare (1 October 1936)
'Are women human?', speaker Dorothy Sayers (14 October 1936)
'French vs English food', Marcel Boulestin (29 October 1936)
'Dramatic criticism: its cause and cure', speaker Ivor Brown (11 December 1936)
Travel film lecture on Switzerland and the Black Forest, speaker John Walker, Thomas Cook (11 February 1937)
'Rhythmic exercise', speaker Mrs Ilse Kroemer (15 February 1937)
'Development of civil aviation', speaker Lawrence Wingfield (16 March 1937)

1937-38

'Fashion secrets', speaker Victor Stiebel, with the collaboration of Norman Hartnell and Digby Morton (22 April 1937)
'Coal under England', speaker Sir Henry Walker, H. M. Chief Inspector of Mines (10 June 1937)
Meeting with Lord Cecil of Chelwood, president of LNSWS (June 1937)
'International peace', speaker Lord Lytton (7 October 1937)
'Life on a farm in south Russia', speaker Miss Delafield (27 October 1937)
'Hospital Savings Association', speaker Mr A. F. Wise (15 November 1937)
'With Shackleton in the Antarctic', speaker Dr L. D. A. Hussey (23 March 1938)

1938-39

Ann Bridge talking on her experiences in China (9 June 1938)
'Penal reform', speaker Alexander Paterson, HM Commissioner of Prisons (10 October 1938)
'From Abraham to Allenby', film, speaker Aidan Crawley (22 November 1938)
'The witch cult', speaker Miss M. A. Murray (25 January 1939)
'Why should non-stop ever stop?', speaker Laura Henderson, founder and owner of the Windmill theatre (22 March 1939)
'The work of the School' (Royal School of Needlework), speaker Lady Smith-Dorrien (26 April 1939)
'Bermuda', film, speaker F. C. Misick (19 July 1939)

Sherry parties:

'The national standard of speech', speaker Elsie Fogerty (14 July 1938)
'Women's Voluntary Services', speaker Lady Reading, chair of WVS (4 October 1938)
'The work of women housing managers', speaker Miss M. E. Hurst (6 December 1938)
'Colour photography', speaker Yevonde (Mrs Middleton) (7 February 1939)
'Women in aviation', speaker Pauline Gower (7 March 1939)
'The ups and downs of a diplomatic correspondent', speaker Madame Geneviève Tabouis, diplomatic correspondent for *L'Œuvre* (24 March 1939)

Other groups clustered round the Junior Council as members explored their particular interests: Arts and Letters, Commerce and Business, Law, Science and Social Work. There was a Debating Society, a Law Group and a Political Group. The Marsham Street Players drew in amateur actors. Musicians played intermittently in the orchestra. Swimming and Walking Groups were also active. The Debating Society got going in 1928, but most groups were at their strongest during the 1930s. Some were short lived, others thrived over a number of years. All of the groups made a point of bringing in outside speakers, some of them distinguished, to their meetings, to stimulate the lively discussion that was a feature of the Junior Council.

Appendix Two

Office-holders of the Fawcett Society and its predecessors

Fawcett chairs
Edith Palliser 1907, London Society for Women's Suffrage
Ray Strachey 1913, London Society for Women's Suffrage
Mrs Kinnell 1919-34, London Society for Women's Service (from 1919)
Elsie Watts 1934-63, London Society for Women's Service; Fawcett Society (from 1953)
Pamela Anderson ?1964
Thelma Cazalet-Keir 1965
Kathleen Halpin 1967-71
Pamela Anderson 1973-77
Mary Smith 1978-79
Mary Stott 1979-82
Betty Scharf 1983-85
Margaret Joachim 1985-87
Sandy Shulman 1987-89
Mary Acland Hood 1989
Annette Lawson 1990-92
Margaret Laird 1992-95
Annette Lawson 1995-96
Jenny Watson 1997-2001
Jane Esuantsiwa Goldsmith 2001-03
Sue Tibballs 2003-05
Michelle Mitchell 2005-07
Angela Mason 2007-13
Belinda Phipps 2013-present

Presidents
Philippa Fawcett 1919, president of London Society for Women's Suffrage
Dame Millicent Garrett Fawcett 1919-29, president of London Society for Women's Service
Viscount Cecil of Chelwood, president of London Society for Women's Service
Lord Bridges, president of Fawcett Society
Baroness Seear 1970-85
Dorothy Wedderburn 1986-2002
Jenni Murray (2003-present)

Senior staff (Directors from 1992)
Shelagh Diplock 1992-98
Mary-Ann Stephenson 1998-2002
Katherine Rake 2002-09
Ceri Goddard 2010-13
Miranda Seymour-Smith 2014
Sam Smethers 2015-

Author's note: These lists have been reconstructed from several sources, and it has not always been possible to verify the strict accuracy of every date. The sequences of office-holders, however, seem clear. In the list of Fawcett chairs the gap between Kathleen Halpin and Pamela Anderson, 1971-73, has not been accounted for.

Appendix Three

Fawcett publications throughout the years

2001-2015

2001	Women and Candidate Selection in British Political Parties
2003	Gender and Poverty
November 2003	Interim Report on Women and Offending: A report on the Fawcett Society's commission on women and the criminal justice system
2004	Money, Money, Money: Is it still a rich man's world?
March 2004	Women and the Criminal Justice System: A report on the Fawcett Society's commission on women and the criminal justice system
February 2005	Black & Minority Ethnic Women in the UK
March 2005	One Year On: Commission on women and the criminal justice system
March 2005	Money, Money, Money: Is it still a rich man's world?
2005	Who Benefits? A gender analysis of the UK benefits and tax credits system
?2006	Justice and Equality: Second annual review of the commission on women and the criminal justice system.
July 2006	Understanding your Duty: Report on the gender equality duty and criminal justice system
July 2006	Doing your Duty: Guide to the gender equality duty
Summer 2006	140 years for Fawcett 1866-2006
July 2007	Women and Justice: Third annual review of the commission on women and the criminal justice system
November 2007	Women's Financial Assets and Debts
March 2008	Seeing Double: Race and gender in ethnic minority women's lives
April 2008	Women and the Future Workplace: A blueprint for change. A Fawcett Society think piece for the launch of the Gender Equality Forum
June 2008	Harnessing the Power of Difference: Race, gender and the future workplace. A Fawcett Society think piece for the launch of the Gender Equality Forum
October 2008	Breaking the Mould for Women Leaders: Could boardroom quotas hold the key? A Fawcett Society think piece for the launch of the Gender Equality Forum

January 2009	Just Below the Surface: Gender stereotyping, the silent barrier to equality in the modern workplace? A Fawcett Society think piece for the launch of the Gender Equality Forum
March 2009	Are Women Bearing the Burden of the Recession?
May 2009	Engendering Justice from Policy to Practice: Final report of the commission on women and the criminal justice system
June 2009	Poverty Pathways: Ethnic minority women's livelihoods
July 2009	Not Having It All: Women's pay and employment prospects
September 2009	Corporate Sexism: The sex industry's infiltration of the modern workplace
November 2009	Closing the Gap: Does transparency hold the key to unlocking pay equality? A Fawcett Society think piece for the launch of the Gender Equality Forum
May 2010	The Business Case for Equal Pay: How the business case for equal pay plays out in practice and what can be done to strengthen it
June 2010	What about Women? Key questions for parliamentarians concerned with advancing women's equality and human rights in the UK
2013	Sex and Power: Who runs Britain?
April 2013	The Changing Labour Market: Delivering for women, delivering for growth
2014	Sex and Power: Who runs Britain?
2015	Where's the Benefit?

Undated publications

Keeping Mum
The New Gender Agenda: Seminar report
Home Truths: An analysis of financial decision making within the home
Sexism and the City: The manifesto, what's rotten in the workplace, and what we can do about it
Red Tape, Red Line: five reasons why government should not "drop its duty" to tackle women's inequality
Equal Pay: Where next?
The Fawcett Charter
Delivering for women? The next steps

Author's note: publications produced by the Fawcett Society's education committee between 1985 and 1990 are listed in Chapter 8, page 124.

Biographies

Elizabeth Garrett Anderson (1836-1917), sister of Millicent Garrett Fawcett, attended school in Blackheath. A close friend of Emily Davies, she campaigned for the entrance of women into higher education, medicine and politics. In 1865 she became the first woman in England to become a licentiate of the Society of Apothecaries; in the same year she helped to found the Kensington Society which contributed to J. S. Mill's suffrage petition. In 1870 she was the first woman to be elected to a London School Board. She developed her own medical practice, launched a new hospital for women, promoted the medical education of women and gave birth to three children. She continued to support the suffrage cause although in 1908 she left the NUWSS to join the WSPU. However, she was to abandon militancy by 1912. In 1908 she became the first woman mayor of Aldeburgh, where she had grown up.

Dame Kathleen Courtney (1878-1974) was active in the suffrage movement, initially as paid secretary of the North of England Society for Women's Suffrage and in 1911 honorary secretary of the NUWSS. At the outbreak of the First World War she was in opposition to many colleagues in the NUWSS who wanted, like Millicent Fawcett, to be involved in war work, and she was one of only three British women who found their way to the International Congress of Women in The Hague in 1915. Out of this came the Women's International League of Peace and Freedom (WILPF) and Kathleen became its first British vice-president in 1916. She also travelled extensively in the Balkans and Poland.

Kathleen rejoined the NUWSS towards the end of the war and was re-elected to the Executive and then to its successor body the National Union of Societies for Equal Citizenship, becoming its vice-president in 1930, and later chaired the Family Endowment Council. She remained passionate about peace and became president of the British branch of WILPF. She was appointed a member of the Executive of the League of Nations, and then in 1939, its vice-chair, travelling the world as a speaker. In 1941 she was elected chair and joint president of the United Nations Association and remained active after retirement. She was created a Dame in 1952.

Vera Douie (1894-1979) OBE was born in India but educated in England. She worked at the War Office Library and on the index of the Medical History of War. She went on to be one of the most renowned librarians of her generation after she became, on 1 January 1926, the first librarian of the London Society for Women's Suffrage. She was to remain in that role with what was to become the Fawcett Library (and subsequently the Women's Library) for forty-one years, and nurtured its growth into what became the foremost depository of women's achievements in the country. During the Second World War she effectively saved the Library by arranging for it to be moved to Oxford and distributed between four different locations.

Vera was active in the wider women's movement and the author of two books *The Lesser Half* (1943) and *Daughters of Britain: An Account of the Work of British Women during the Second World War* (1950). She was awarded the OBE for her life's work when she retired in 1967.

John Stuart Mill (1806-1873), political economist and philosopher, had a long-held belief that the legal subordination of one sex to another was wrong, singling out sexual equality as being one of the important aspects of socialism. He believed in 'the greatest happiness of the greatest number' – and he definitely included women in that number! Mill worked closely with his step-daughter Helen Taylor on the advancement of women and was a friend of Henry Fawcett. In 1869 he published *The Subjection of Women* jointly with Helen Taylor. From 1865 to 1868, he served as Member of Parliament for the Westminster constituency and was widely known as the parliamentary champion of women's enfranchisement. Millicent Fawcett became politicised by attending one of Mill's election meetings. In 1866, with Parliament discussing the Reform Bill, Mill declared himself happy to present a petition in favour of women's suffrage on behalf of the Women's Suffrage Petition Committee (although this was unsuccessful). Other petitions followed. Mill lost his Westminster seat in 1868, but all his life he remained active in suffrage and feminist politics, for example, sponsoring the Married Women's Property Bill in 1868.

Mary Stott (1907-2002) OBE was one of the most famous campaigning journalists of the twentieth century in Britain. She was both the first and the longest-serving (1957-72) editor of the *Guardian* Women's page, making it a platform for women's voices and concerns. She also used it as the means to establish new organisations like the Housewives' Register and the Pre-school Playgroups Association.

Mary's life in Fawcett began when she retired and came to live in London. She was an active member both of Women in Media and Fawcett's media committee. She was chair of Fawcett 1979-81 and organised the Women's Action Day in November 1980. She was always a passionate supporter of the Library. Her most famous books are *Forgetting's No Excuse* (1973) (about bereavement) and *Before I Go* (1985) about old age. She was passionate about painting and singing (singing bass in old age) and delighted to be awarded three honorary degrees.

Philippa Strachey (1872-1968), sister of Lytton and sister-in-law of Ray, came from a famous family (she was the last surviving member of the ten distinguished Strachey siblings) but became renowned in her own right for her contribution to the women's movement and particularly to what was to become the Fawcett Society. She was the organiser of the first great women's suffrage procession – the Mud March – in 1907, the year she became secretary of the London Society for Women's Suffrage. She held that post until 1951 and for another decade supported the Society as honorary secretary. She fought for equal pay, and campaigned to open the professions to women and to secure complete equality for women in the Civil Service. She was involved both in Bedford College, London and Newnham College, Cambridge, and served on the Appointments Committee of Cambridge University. At her death Duncan Grant and Leonard Woolf were asked to write appreciations. In Mary Stocks' words, 'she was a vital and constant force at the centre of the constitutional women's movement'.

Ray Strachey (1887-1940), daughter of the suffragist Mary Costelloe and wife of Oliver Strachey, was educated at Newnham College, Cambridge (1905-08), where she became involved in suffrage politics. She took part in a suffrage tour of the Lake District. In 1913 she was chair of the London Society for Women's Suffrage (LSWS). From 1916 to 1921 she was honorary parliamentary secretary of NUWSS, responsible for supervising the passage of the 1918 Reform Bill, and was also active in the Women's Service Bureau, which originated in the war work of LSWS. She acted as political private secretary to Lady Astor, when she became the first woman MP. Ray herself stood unsuccessfully for parliament three times, as an independent. After the First World War she was editor of *The Common Cause* and its successor *Women's Leader*. Ray's books include *Women's Suffrage and Women's Service: The History of the London and National Society for Women's Service* (1927), *The Cause: A Short History of the Women's Movement in Great Britain* (1928), a biography of *Millicent Garrett Fawcett* (1931), *Careers and Openings for Women* (1935) and *Our Freedom and its Results*, a collection of essays by five women she edited, published in 1936 by Virginia and Leonard Woolf's Hogarth Press.

59. *At the beginning of its anniversary year Fawcett published a major Report* Sex Equality: State of the Nation 2016 *which asked 8,000 people about their views on gender equality. Note Fawcett's new logo to celebrate its anniversary year*

Sex Equality ▶▶
State of the Nation 2016

Index